QUESTIONS
NOT BEING ASKED

**TOPICAL PHILOSOPHICAL CRITIQUES IN PROSE,
PROVERBS, AND POEMS**

Inno Chukuma Onwueme

authorHOUSE®

AuthorHouse™
1663 Liberty Drive
Bloomington, IN 47403
www.authorhouse.com
Phone: 1 (800) 839-8640

Published by AuthorHouse 05/05/2015

ISBN: 978-1-5049-0988-4 (sc)
ISBN: 978-1-5049-0987-7 (e)

Library of Congress Control Number: 2015906862

Print information available on the last page.

DEDICATION

To the memory of Baba and Mama, my parents

To my grandchildren: Soli, Kaiyo, Jido, Malobi,
NwaMalije, and others coming later

To the obsolescence of War as an activity
that civilized humans undertake

To Warlessness

To PEACE

CONTENTS

ACKNOWLEDGMENT

I acknowledge, with thanks, all those who have contributed to the genesis of this book, directly or indirectly. I thank Eric Eckert, Bundo Onwueme, Malije Onwueme, and Chimaobi Chijioke for proofreading the early drafts. To Keno Onwueme, I am grateful for permission to illustrate the book with his artwork.

This book is intended as a philosophical distillation from my life experiences. In that sense, it has been shaped by all the co-travelers that I've encountered throughout my life. I'm grateful to all of them. Looking back, I am moved to say:

> **"... For all of life, the pleasing and the hateful,**
> **To God Almighty, I am most grateful."**
> *(modified from I.C. Onwueme poem, 1994)*

INTRODUCTION

After a long languid night, the tropical meadow hangs heavy with high humidity. Like the stylized formless clouds at the dawn of creation, most objects in the meadow are hazy in the diffuse darkness left over from the night. Very soon, a suffused glow of light from the eastern horizon begins to bathe earth and sky. Dimly at first, but then getting progressively brighter. Birds are already chirping energetically, announcing that the big solar giant is about to stir from its slumber. The giant itself is not yet visible, but its aura is unmistakable. Its glow is already livening up the spirits in the animal and plant realms. All living things are abuzz in anticipation of a new day.

In one corner of the meadow, a flower bud, tightly clenched in reclusive posture for the past many weeks, is finally unfurling its beautiful face to the world. And what a beauty it is to behold. It's a treat not for the sight alone, but all olfactory organs nearby are assailed by its pleasant aroma. And that's not all it has to offer. Ensconced deep within its being is a package of sweet, energizing nectar. This flower offers the complete triple package for the eyes, the nostrils, and the palate. All this offering is an enticement for all kinds of insects to visit. "I'm available to be pollinated," the flower says. "And while you're at it, I will reward you with my triple package."

During the course of this day, before the sun goes to sleep again, this attractive package will have lured all kinds of insect visitors to come by. Butterflies, bees, flies, wasps, moths, and many kinds of flying insects all line up for their turn to visit. Some visits are uneventful, resulting only in the visitor partaking of the triple package and saying goodbye. A free lunch, you might say. But other visits are hugely significant, since the visitors bring the potent present of pollen, mostly from other sources, to pollinate the flower. The result is the formation of a seed. A seed that will mature and later germinate to produce the next generation.

A human mind in contemplative solitude is like the flower in the meadow. It sings out, "I'm available to be pollinated." Many thoughts and ideas flutter around, visit for brief moments, and are again on their way. In that sense, many of the visits are fleeting and unproductive, especially if their essence has not been captured. However, some of the visits are profound enough to be captured, nurtured, and made productive. They grow into the seeds that give rise to other thoughts and imaginings.

This book is essentially a chronicle of some of the thoughts that came to my mind over a period of a quarter century, from about 1989 to 2014. It was a period in my life when I enjoyed considerable stretches of solitude. My mind was like a flower in the meadow, lying in wait for productive pollinators to perch. This situation permitted a great deal of introspection and rumination which explored trains of thought that I would not otherwise have contemplated or countenanced. There is no telling which of these thoughts may have previously been thought or recorded by others. But to the extent that they have arisen independently in my mind, I can claim my share of ownership of them.

Since many profound thoughts are fleeting, I formed the habit of committing them to paper as soon as they struck me. I meticulously kept a journal in which I elaborated each thought, along with the place and date on which the entry was made. Many times, I would interrupt a meal, a television program, or siesta, so I could reach for my journal to write down a fleeting thought. That journal has been indispensable as I've tried to compile this book at the end of the period, with only minor updating and editing. In a sense, each journal entry was a historical record of the thoughts that were being thought by a particular person at a particular place and time. For this reason, many of the items in this book are accompanied by the date and place where each item was originally written. Some of the dates and places may seem repetitive, but they are essential for preserving the historical nature of this work.

Needless to say, the thoughts ranged from the profound to the profane, and varied considerably in quality. But a crocodile sitting patiently in the river shallows does not scurry after every passing animal or fish. It is selective. Similarly, not all my journal entries and thoughts have risen to the level of being worthy to be shared. Many have been left out. Some other thoughts may have been profound at the time they were recorded, but have lost relevance due to subsequent events or changed circumstances. In a few cases, my own views may have moved on since the thought was first recorded. However, I'm gratified to note that many of the thoughts have retained their relevance into the next quarter century, and a few look set to endure well beyond that. In any case, the selection process has enabled some very unique thoughts and ideas to filter through and bubble up to the surface. Ideas that I have never thought of before; ideas that I have never heard of before. Questions that public discourse has deemed unpleasant and unpalatable. Questions that are conveniently avoided or ignored. In short, questions that are not being asked.

Why are these questions not being asked in public discourse, especially since some of them seem so obvious? Part of the reason, I think, is due to fawning, uncurious timidity that obliges most people (including the mass media) to stay within the narrow straightjacket of received paradigms. The unquestioning attitude is driven by a quirky concept of patriotism and a desperate need to conform. We forget that the greatest disservice you can do to patriotism is to let societal ills fester unchallenged; and that the greatest service you can do to it is to critique the good that exists in order to make it better.

While social media have their role in society, the traditional integrity of mass media journalism has, of late, been seriously swamped and eroded by the tremendous trove of trite detritus flooding in from social media outlets. This is more so since these outlets, thanks to modern technology, now have a capacity for rapid virulence that was hitherto not possible. The transition from traditional newsgathering to crowd-sourced news is still in progress, and is froth with imperfections. Whether oral or electronic, cheap inexpensive talk threatens to replace deep pensive thought. The volume is high, but the quality and veracity are not necessarily so. The voice of the majority is so loud and overwhelming that the minority opinion, even if true, is drowned out and forced to cower for cover in the shadows. Facilitated by mass electronic communication, there is a stampeding herd instinct that obliges most people to head in the same direction as the herd. It is a self-propelling "me too" treadmill hysteria that unquestioningly pushes everybody in the same politically correct direction as everybody else.

The events in the United States of America (US) that led up to the Iraq war provide a classic example. The US mass media were obsequiously flaunting their patriotism but flouting their professional ethics. They were eager to embrace the falsehood that their government was dishing out to them, and to superciliously dismiss, with mocking no less, the truth that the United Nations was speaking. Professional tepidity would not let them ask the questions that were not being asked, the questions that would have led them to the truth. Similarly, daily network news and talk-show interviews, especially with government officials, are often characterized by a fawning patronizing approach that only amplifies the one-sided views of the interviewee. Obvious questions that contradict the ongoing popular narrative are carefully avoided so as to preserve and reinforce the preferred narrative. The watchdog role of the media is not always in evidence. Unfortunately, when the watchdogs are asleep in the hay, the mad dogs have a field day. With the mass media often failing to ask the tough questions, the questions not being asked are denied a place in shaping public opinion.

I cannot claim to have answers to many of the questions raised in this book. I do not. But I believe that the questions should at least be dangled as bait for public discourse to chomp on. Hopefully, the disparate answers proffered by various people may eventually lead to resolution.

Much of this work is a commentary on the period's burning issues: global, national, local, and personal. While some entries comment on global geopolitics, others mark specific events in my personal or professional life. In addition, many of the pieces relate to the timeless universal human condition, with commentaries on war/peace, love, spirituality, environmental sustainability, consumerism, and the rights of individuals. As such, the moods of the pieces range from deeply philosophical to critical, to whimsical, to humorous. This eclectic collection bears testimony to how widely a curious mind can range in its effort to remain aware and engaged in its surroundings.

Some parts of this book are inevitably critical of certain nations, notions, and traditions. In a few cases, hyperbole has been used to get the point across. The intent here is not to derogate or denigrate. Instead, all the criticisms are offered in good faith, on the presumption that the catharsis of criticism ultimately leads to reflection and refinement. Like criticism directed at a brother, the sentiment is one of love with corrective intent, not hate with vituperative intent. As indicated in some sections, even I and my relatives are culpable when it comes to some of the issues raised. The precepts that I have tried to foster are intended as aspirational benchmarks. My goal has been to evoke debate that will ultimately lead to improvement of that which is criticized. The item may already be good, but constructive criticism makes it even better. I apologize in advance for any displeasure that my criticisms may cause. Given the wide range of topics, and the nature of opinionated commentary, I expect most readers of this book to find at least one view that they agree with, and at least one with which they disagree. This should not come as a surprise, or be cause for animated agitation. Such is the nature of intellectual discourse and disputation.

As each thought came to mind, I allowed myself a choice of the literary format in which to express it. The most detailed thoughts were elaborated into full-length essays (Section A), or were condensed into poetry (Sections B and D). Briefer thoughts are laid out as "rantings" and aphorisms (Section C). This use of diverse formats makes the book richer and more engaging. It offers the reader a cornucopian plate for the adventurous palate.

Where generic gender references such as "him/her" occur in this work, I have mostly opted to use either "him" or "her", on the understanding that the other gender is equally represented. Hopefully, this makes for smoother reading than constantly repeating "him/her" or "he/she".

Going on forty years since I authored my first major book, I plan to resist the temptation to embark on another book project in future.

After authoring about a dozen books (mostly in my area of expertise of agricultural science/sustainability), I envisage that this will be the last of my books before I put my pen out to dry. I see this book as a summative capstone effort that draws on the philosophical aggregation and accretion of my life experiences. I welcome you to join me in exploring some aspects of our being that transcend all academic disciplines.

The drawings that appear inside this book were done by Dr. Kenolisa Onwueme (my son). They are reproduced with his permission and my gratitude. The drawings shown here are being published for the first time, and form part of a larger collection by the same amateur artist. All were originally done as doodles, on scraps of paper, as his way to distract himself from the rigors of medical school.

SECTION A:

PHILOSOPHICAL ESSAYS AND INSIGHTS

[In sequence: Social, Philosophical, Spiritual, Political, War/Peace]

1

The Civil Union Debate: A creative solution with no losers

__Context__: In the first two decades of the 21st century, the world has been roiled by the debate over same-sex relationships. This debate has been particularly acrimonious in western society, especially the USA. As often happens, the debate has been framed in the paradigm of winners and losers. This essay, written between August 2006 and June 2012 while living in the USA, contributes to the debate by suggesting a solution with no losers.

Who has not heard of the debate surrounding the union of one person with another of the same sex? Unless you've been living on another planet, you could not have missed the roaring rumpus. Virtually everybody on earth has been part of the debate or been affected by it. Over the past half century, this debate has generated a dizzying amount of friction and heat in many parts of the world. The issue is red-hot in many countries. Politicians who dare to touch it generate an unforgiving sizzle that, once felt, scares them away. Religious officials fare no better. At the same time, the controversy is scorching through the general population, leaving beleaguered segments of society isolated from one another by large patches of charred ethical wasteland. This issue alone has spawned a whole series of court rulings, state constitutional amendments, and bitter acrimony in the polity all over America. It looms large as one of the markers in the cultural divide that agitates the US in the early years of the twenty-first century.

One plane of the debate is whether or not the state should recognize homosexual relationships and accord the partners the same civil privileges as are currently bestowed on heterosexual married couples. The other plane of the debate seeks to restrict the definition of marriage to something which can only occur between a man and a woman. In that context, homosexual relationships could not qualify as marriage, and would not carry the civil privileges that accrue to married heterosexual couples. This essay attempts to analyze some of the issues involved, and suggests a way forward not only for the USA, but also for western society as a whole.

By current societal norms in the western world, marriage bestows on the partners two different sets of privileges: sexual privileges and social/civil privileges. The sexual privilege consists of unfettered reasonable sexual access to each other, and in most cases, the attendant joint effort at procreation. The civil privilege consists of such things as inheritance rights, property ownership, joint taxation, mutual rights of attorney/deputation in cases of incapacitation, and several other mutual obligations or rights that may vary slightly from country to country. These two sets of privileges are understood to accrue automatically and simultaneously to married heterosexual couples.

Western society and most of the world already grant homosexual pairs unfettered sexual privilege with each other. Very few western societies proscribe homosexual pairing. The crux of the debate about homosexual unions is that while homosexual partners are free to enjoy the sexual privilege, they are often denied the civil privileges. So, indeed, the main theater of the debate is in the area of the civil privilege.

The sexual and civil privileges are invariably linked, and are bestowed together in heterosexual marriages in most western societies. This seems ideal. But are these two privileges inexorably and organically linked? Must they be linked? Can they be separated? Is it possible that this linking of sexual and civil privileges is the source of much of the crisis surrounding the ongoing civil union debate?

The search for a solution to the civil union debate leads me to make a proposal which I call the *Privileges Separation Proposal* (PSP for short). I propose that society agrees to de-link the civil privilege from the sexual privilege in all circumstances, including heterosexual marriage. Irrespective of who shares their sexual privilege, each adult would be free and entitled to choose any one adult in the society with whom to share his/her civil privilege. Furthermore, only the civil privilege would attract state recognition/documentation; while the sexual privilege would remain completely private, outside the purview of the state. Let me now elaborate on this proposal.

Let us refer to the person chosen to share the civil privilege as the *civil delegate*. The partners in a heterosexual marriage would, by choice, hopefully designate each other as the mutual and reciprocal beneficiaries of their civil privilege. But they don't necessarily have to. They could conceivably each choose somebody else as their civil delegate. When civil and sexual privileges are de-linked, even single persons who are not in any kind of relationship are free to choose anyone they like with whom to share their civil privilege. And because this privilege is devoid of sexual content, the person they choose does not have to be an actual or potential sexual partner. It could even be a brother or sister. And coming to the contentious issue of the homosexual relationship, the partners would now be free to choose each other (or not) for the state-recognized civil privileges. All of a sudden, the playing field for civil privileges becomes equitably level for the heterosexual, homosexual, or single persons. The wind is taken out of the sail of the debate about state recognition of homosexual relationships, since the sexual aspect of *all* relationships ceases to attract state recognition.

In this scheme, the state takes itself out of the business of recognizing or not recognizing a person's sexual privileges, choices, or preferences. The state confines itself to recognizing and acknowledging people's bestowed choices of civil delegates. And such bestowal is without prejudice to whether or not sexual privileges are bestowed at the same time. The state would not register the combined package of sexual and civil privileges (marriage as traditionally defined), but would only register each person's declaration of who their "civil delegate" is for civil privileges. Each adult would have only one civil delegate at any one time, but would be free to make changes from time to time. When it comes to sexual privileges, the state would stay out of that turf completely, deferring instead to religious bodies. In contrast to the state, religious organizations ("church" for short) would remain free to recognize or bless sexual unions, with each church free to draw the line as to which sexual union it wishes to bless or abhor.

A sub-set of the civil union debate is whether the term "marriage" should include the union between single-sex couples. In other words, should the term "marriage" be exclusively for the union between a man and a woman? This debate is not trivial. It has risen to the level of evoking a debated bill in the US Congress that would amend the US Constitution to define marriage as being exclusively between a man and a woman. Many states in the US have debated, and in some cases passed, similar measures. On the one hand, you could argue that the term marriage has, for millennia, been used to describe a man-woman union, and that any other kind of union (even if it conveys the same or even more privileges) should bear some other name. On the other hand, it could be argued that any union that carries the same sexual and civil privileges as marriage should be described as marriage. But in the final analysis, is this not just a debate over semantics? Whichever way the semantics debate is pushed, the core demand of the gay rights movement is to have the same privileges (rights) as heterosexual married couples. The name that is used for their kind of union is slightly secondary. They want a package of civil privileges linked (coupled) with their sexual privilege, just as it is for heterosexuals. But if you de-link the two sets of privileges for everybody as I now propose, then there's an even playing field for all. Everybody can enjoy the same civil privileges in the public domain, without the public peering into their bedroom behavior. Everybody's sexual behavior and preferences remain out of sight and are confined to the private domain. Indeed, a gay union, by whatever name, could theoretically have more, the same, or less civil and sexual privileges than the conventional heterosexual marriage.

When each adult is free to designate any other adult as their civil delegate to bear their civil privilege, most pairs of individuals would probably agree to mutually designate each other as such. That is, I designate you as my civil delegate and you designate me as yours. But the mutuality of the designation is not a pre-requisite. While the ideal is for mutual designation, person A could designate person B, while person B could theoretically designate somebody else. One would expect that heterosexual married couples, and even homosexual partners, would mutually designate each other as civil delegates. But they could, by mutual understanding, each designate someone else (e.g. a relative). The main caveat in such cases is to ensure that the interests of children are protected (similar to the way children's interests are protected in today's system with its high divorce and re-marriage rates).

What does the Privileges Separation Proposal do to the "sanctity" of marriage? Let's look at two different heterosexual couples. One couple gets married in the church, but precede their marriage with a prenuptial agreement that basically prescribes that they have very limited civil/property privileges over each other. Would the church authorities consider that the sanctity of marriage has been violated? Most probably not, even though the couple's relationship is heavy on sexual privilege but thin on civil privileges. Now, let's look at another couple. They live together, own everything together, do everything together, etc., but refuse to get formally married, despite well-meaning entreaties from relatives. Would the church authorities consider that the sanctity of marriage has been violated? Most probably yes, despite the strength of the civil privileges that this couple share. The main point here is that the religious authorities, who are the ultimate guardians of sanctity, are much more concerned with the bestowal of the sexual privilege, and it is only to a lesser degree that they are interested in the civil privilege. In the PSP, the state would abdicate its oversight of the sexual privilege, leaving the church with unfettered influence in this sphere. This just happens to be the sphere that religious groups are most interested in. The sanctity of marriage is not violated and everybody wins. Indeed, with the PSP, the term marriage could become the exclusive preserve of the religiously-mediated union (hetero or homo) which would have no larger civil consequences *per se*. The civil privileges, if they are to be shared by the same couple, would be a separate transaction with the state.

Where does *love* figure into all this? Each kind of privilege and its bestowal is indeed an act of love. In the case of the sexual privilege, it is essentially romantic/carnal love. In the case of the civil privilege, it could be romantic or other kinds of love. Most people in genuine committed relationships probably would voluntarily and reciprocally bestow both kinds of privileges on each other as the ultimate act of romantic and non-romantic love. And the same love permeates to the children that grow up under the umbrella of that relationship.

The civil union debate has often been cast in a *civil rights* context. If the heterosexual married couple can have civil privileges linked to their sexual privileges, why should the homosexual couple be denied the same? Why can't the gay man jointly own a house or jointly file tax returns or have survivor benefits with his partner, when the heterosexual married man can do so with his spouse. Surely, the civil rights of the gay man are being violated. The expectation is that granting the gay person those same civil privileges will clinch the argument, restore their civil rights, and all will be well.

Now let's examine the civil rights argument a bit more closely. The expected end game is when both heterosexual and homosexual couples can have their civil privileges recognized. The cause of civil rights would have been served. Sure. Sure? Not so fast. Recall that one unique characteristic of "civil rights" is that it is applicable to the entire adult population. Once the argument is based on it, we open up a whole new theater of discourse. When all coupled adults (homo and hetero) have been served, where does that leave adults who are single by choice or by circumstance?

This is not an insignificant slice of the population. To this singles group belong the preponderant majority of college students and most of their age-mates who did not go to college. The recent trend of waiting and marrying later also means that there is a whole sea of single pre-marriage adults well beyond college-age years. Then there is the increasing rate of divorce in society which in itself throws up a large number of post-marriage adults who are temporarily or permanently single at any given time. The same is true of widows and widowers who opt not to remarry. Then there is the large number of persons who remain deliberately celibate for religious, social, or other reasons. Indeed, in 2010, about 43% of all Americans over the age of 18 were single, according to the U.S. Census Bureau. Of this group, 61% never married, 24% were divorced, and 15% were widowed. That's a total of some 96 million persons! Does this significant segment of the population deserve to have civil privileges as well? Can any two of them file joint tax returns or have survivor benefits without giving up their singlehood? Are they not being denied the civil rights enjoyed by persons in coupled "marriage" (hetero, and homo)? Is society forcing those who have chosen to be single into some sort of marriage in order for them to be entitled to share their civil privileges?

The point is that the present marriage system has no answers to most of the questions above. Even if you legalize homosexual marriages on the basis of civil rights, you still leave a huge segment of the population (singles) disenfranchised. How do you cater to the civil rights of the singles? I posit that the Privileges Separation Proposal above provides an answer. It does so by de-linking civil privileges from sexual privileges, and asking the state to only recognize civil privileges. The bestowal of the civil privilege is then available to any individual whether hetero-married, homo-married, never married, divorced, or widowed. The state remains neutral to your marital status, and permits you to select any adult individual with whom you wish to share your civil privileges. That is the only way civil rights can be served all across the board.

The solution offered above may be long in coming or never at all. If so, the agitation for the civil rights of singles may be the next theater in America's ever-shifting social battleground.

In summary, the Privileges Separation Proposal has several advantages:

- *Take the state out of sexual recognition:* It enables the state to take a neutral position with respect to the sexual coupling that people get into. Among other things, this saves us from the current Orwellian intrusiveness by the state into people's sexual activities, an intrusiveness which most of us have long accepted unquestioningly. The state is relieved of the responsibility of recognizing (or not) the sexual pairing behavior of the adult populace, while still giving recognition to people's freely-chosen beneficiaries of their civil privileges. In an era when people are keen to minimize the role of "government" in their lives, most people will welcome an end to the current role of the state in people's sexuality. Incidentally, the current agitation of the gay movement is towards parity of state recognition of homosexual and heterosexual relationships. The agitation is for the state to recognize and register homosexual marriages/unions, just as it has long recognized heterosexual marriages. If anything, this draws the state deeper into the business of recognizing people's sexuality. What I propose here is a disentangling solution in the opposite direction: the state disengages from its current intrusion into the sexual privileges of heterosexual couples, rather than adding on the same role for homosexual couples.

- *Grant individuals greater freedom of choice:* The PSP permits a greater freedom of choice for the individual, even to the extent where their sexual privilege and their civil privilege could theoretically go in different directions. What do we make of the boom in prenuptial agreements in recent years? Are they not simply an attempt to separate the civil privilege away from the sexual privilege, and to modify the civil privilege in whatever way the partners deem fit? Such arrangements are only one step away from the system of free choice in the bestowal of the civil privilege, as proposed here.

- *Take the heat out of the debate about same-sex unions:* One huge benefit of the PSP is that the raging debate about state recognition of homosexual unions is rendered completely moot. All the heat and fury, all the attempts to amend centuries-old constitutions, all the state by state referendums, all the huffing and puffing between homophiliacs and homophobiacs; all that will be stilled by the onset of the new PSP system. It provides a level playing field where the state is neutral about your sexuality.

- *Demystify private sexual behavior:* The PSP will demystify cohabitation arrangements that have varying degrees of sexual content: from heterosexual "church-married" couples, to single man and woman living together, to same-sex persons living together, etc. All would be legally equal in the sense that none of them would attract any sign of documentation, approval, or rejection by the state. The state would be neutral in these matters, just as the state does not have to exercise an opinion into whether I wear blue shirts on Tuesdays, or use mustard on my hamburgers.

- *Strengthen the role of religious and social organizations:* The PSP actually strengthens the role of religious organizations by preserving their right to moralize over the appropriate context for bestowing sexual privileges. Just as now, each couple would be free to subject their union to the strictures of a religious organization of their choice. Such a wedding is strictly a religious event, with none of the civic overtones that exist in the present system. It would be akin to what happens now when a couple who did a registry marriage years ago decide to do a church wedding. The adoption of the PSP system is unlikely to decrease the numbers of religious weddings. Even non-religious people would still be free to do a social wedding ceremony, but the state's role in it is only to register their voluntary bestowal of civil benefits on each other. If the bestowal has been registered earlier, or is destined for other persons, then there is no state intrusion whatsoever into the ensuing celebrations. The current system entangles the church in the strictly secular matter of distributing civil privileges; the PSP frees the church from the issue of civil privileges, enabling it to concentrate on the moral turf of sexual privileges which is its main concern. The PSP more clearly demarcates the roles for state and church in the union of two adults: the state deals with civil privileges; the church deals with sexual privileges.

- *Do not exclude singles in the civil rights protections:* The PSP provides equal civil rights protections for all categories of persons, including singles.

The acrimony over same-sex relationships has been increasing for years, and the trend is likely to continue. Politicians and religious pundits have had a field day whipping up their partisans on one side or the other of the debate. Partly for this reason, and partly for reasons of inertia resulting from millennia of habit, it will not be easy to change the paradigms that we use for matters of sex and marriage. My Privileges Separation Proposal is not perfect and is bound to be controversial. But it does offer a new beginning for restoring societal harmony to an area of our lives where harmony is most needed. And it does so while avoiding the zero-sum paradigm of winners and losers. Think about it.

2

Mother-Tongue Needs Mothering, Not Smothering: Enthroning the mother-tongue in the home

<u>Context</u>: Originally written in 1992 in Owerri, Nigeria. Edited in 2013.

All over the world, the phenomenon of language *abandonment* at the family level is precipitating a crisis of language *extinction* at the larger community level. From India to the Americas, from the Congo basin to Papua New Guinea, from Indonesia to Nigeria, many indigenous languages are being lost due to neglect, exacerbated by the insidious intrusion of the world's major languages. Just as species extinction deprives the world of its biological heritage, language extinction abrasively erodes the world's cultural heritage. The genesis of this erosion lies within individual families. The seeds of decay lie secretly buried in the home.

Let's say you are living in New York. You are an indigene of the Anioma ethnic group in Nigeria, and you are proud of it. Congratulations! Your spouse, too, is from Anioma. Congratulations again. Before you came over to the U.S.A., you resided in Lagos, outside the Anioma ethnic area, and all your four children were born there. During those years in Lagos, and up till now, your family's domestic language in the home has been English. Now none of your children can speak your Anioma language. Their mates at school do not even believe them when they say they are from Anioma, since they cannot back up the claim with the required language skills. So, wherein lies their claim to being Anioma indigenes? Where have they failed? Where have you failed in your parenting?

18

No, you have not failed; at least judging from the fact that you've got plenty of company. Many other parents in the US and Nigeria are in the same awkward position. So too are parents from many other countries around the world who find that they have failed to pass on their native language to their children, and that they are the last generation in their line to speak the language. They have given birth to linguistic eunuchs, stranded in a linguistic dead-end.

Let's use the Nigerian parents as an example, since their situation has similarities in many other countries around the world. It is amazing these days to observe the number of Nigerian families that use English as the means of communication within the home (i.e. the domestic language). This is particularly so among the middle and upper class families, who sometimes give the impression that their claim to modernity is reinforced by the use of English as the domestic language.

The position of the English language in Nigerian officialdom is clear and unassailable. It is the one official language that permits communication between the various parts and segments of the multi-ethnic multi-lingual country. In most urban centers, with their mix of various ethnic/linguistic groups, the English language (or adaptations from it) also serves as the common medium of expression on the street. The use of English to communicate among persons with different mother-tongues is most certainly borne out of necessity. Its use in these circumstances can be said to be obligatory. In contrast, the use of English within the home is very often elective, especially in situations where both parents originate from the same linguistic group. The elective use of English within the home exists in virtually all ethnic groups in the country. It is only for purposes of illustration that this discussion focuses on the Anioma people. Otherwise, the discussion is just as applicable to other ethnic and linguistic groups in Nigeria, and even in the world generally.

Let us start by considering the simplest situation where husband and wife are both from Anioma, and the children, by derivation, are also Anioma indigenes (i.e. the family is mono-ethnic). There is a commonality of origin and language for the entire family. It is surprising that even in such a situation, many families can be found using English as the domestic language. Surely, there is a crass incongruity in a situation where father, mother, and children collectively conspire to abandon their common linguistic heritage, and opt to communicate with one another in a tongue that is alien to every one of them. One would have to search quite hard to find a Japanese man married to a Japanese woman of the same linguistic extraction, adopting some other language for intra-familial communication. The same could be said of Germans, Tongans, Vietnamese, and many ethnic groups around the world. But in Nigeria and in many post-colonial societies, the situation is different.

Let us now take a critical and analytical look at how a nuclear family comes to adopt the mother-tongue (or English or any other language) as the domestic language of the home. The seeds of the pattern are sown very early in the life of the nuclear family, usually when the couple are still alone and the children are yet to arrive. If the spouses communicate with each other in their mother-tongue, they are able to initiate the first child/dependent into the practice. A critical mass of Anioma speakers would have been formed. Subsequent additions to the family (children or wards) simply follow the existing pattern, and unwittingly enlarge the pool of Anioma speakers. Soon, the presence of the parents is no longer necessary for the children to continue using the mother-tongue within the home. As the group enlarges, it gathers a momentum of its own, and the domestic language becomes entrenched and self-perpetuating. Dislodging the entrenched domestic language to substitute another becomes progressively more difficult as time goes on and the family group enlarges. Once the domestic linguistic compass is set early in one direction, it becomes difficult to re-set in another direction. So, whether it is the mother-tongue, English, or any other language that takes hold as the domestic language early in the life of the family, making a change later on may prove extremely difficult.

The language of communication between husband and wife in the early stages of marriage is therefore critical in determining the life-long domestic language of the family. This also reveals how the adoption of English as the domestic language comes about in many mono-ethnic Nigerian families. One of the spouses, perhaps lacking adequate grounding in their mother-tongue, may be more comfortable communicating in English in the home. The other spouse obliges, eager not to offend. Then the first child obliges; subsequent children oblige; wards and live-in relatives oblige. The stage is set for life-long use of English as the domestic language, producing a generation of children that are effectively shut out from their supposed mother-tongue.

In most instances, the use of English as the domestic language is not arrived at by deliberate reasoned choice. It simply comes about by default, but is permitted or tolerated by the family members. There is little or no conscious evaluation of the relative advantages of using English as opposed to the mother-tongue as the domestic language. Such a cavalier attitude to choosing the domestic language presupposes that there are no far-reaching consequences of choosing English instead of the mother-tongue to serve as the domestic language. The risks implicit in this assumption will be addressed later.

Even in cases where the nuclear family is ostensibly mono-ethnic and mono-linguistic, a strong tendency to ethnic pluralism can come through the influence of nannies or child-minders. If the child-minder, whether resident or part-time, is of a different linguistic extraction from the rest of the family, she invariably communicates with the child in the home in English. This establishes a beach-head for the promotion of English as the domestic language. Everybody else in the family is obliged to communicate with the child minder in English, and vice versa. If the child-minder is of the full-time live-in type, there is a heightened frequency and intensity of this inevitable communication in English in the home. The beach-head for English as the domestic language is thus enlarged significantly, while the family's mother-tongue is progressively occluded. The family is now in a dilemma: either operate in two different languages (i.e. English and the mother-tongue), or take the easy way out and use English alone as the domestic language. As implied already, the second option is the easier one and many families choose it uncritically. Only a few families are able to insist on retaining the mother-tongue. However, the ability to achieve this depends on the willingness and ability of the parents to spend a good proportion of their time with the children. This requirement cannot easily be met by many working executive parents. They just cannot match the long hours that the child-minder spends with the child each day, all the time communicating in English. The child-minder is therefore a very potent influence in pushing the family towards the adoption of English as the domestic language. Her influence can, in fact, subvert and subdue the initial efforts of the young couple to retain their mother-tongue as the domestic language.

The adoption of English as the domestic language can, therefore, arise from one spouse being uncomfortable with the mother-tongue, or from the insidious influence of a child-minder who hails from another linguistic group. A third predisposing situation for the mono-ethnic nuclear family is where such a family lives outside their own linguistic area. This could be within the same country (e.g. the Anioma indigene living in Lagos), or in another country. In such cases, English is the language of communication for the children at school and on the street (including when they are at play with the neighborhood children). Such a large part of their day is spent communicating in English that its importation into the home to serve as the domestic language is only a matter of time. Such pressures are particularly strong in cosmopolitan multi-ethnic cities such as Warri, Lagos, Port Harcourt, or Jos, where a form of English is the language on the street. Similar pressures also exist for mono-ethnic families living overseas (e.g. the Anioma indigenes living in New York). Parents in such families require a tremendous amount of effort if they desire to ward off the encroachment of English into the home.

For the truly mono-ethnic Anioma family, one argument in favor of English as the domestic language is that since English is the country's lingua franca, its use at home (as well as in school) enhances the child's proficiency in it. Even if this argument is valid, one may ask: at what cost is this additional proficiency being achieved? If the child speaks English at school, and also English in the home, where, one may ask, is he supposed to acquire proficiency in his mother-tongue? This question is particularly poignant for the child living outside his native linguistic area (in-country or overseas), since English may also be the language of the street, in addition to being that of school and home.

Proficiency in English is a worthy goal; but so also is proficiency in the mother-tongue. The achievement of one must not be at the expense of the other. Indeed, social anthropologists tell us that language is not just a means of communication: it also influences our thought processes, our world view, and our cultural perspective. Our mother-tongue is therefore not just a means of communicating with others; it is a condensed package of our cultural being. It is our most significant identity symbol to prove our membership of our claimed ethnic group. Therefore, a child who is denied proficiency in his mother-tongue is simultaneously denied an important aspect of the culture of his people. Some would go so far as to assert that proficiency in the mother-tongue is an inalienable right of every child, and is indispensable for his normal cultural development.

Once we are convinced of the need for the child to acquire proficiency in his mother-tongue, we must ensure that the opportunity for such acquisition is presented. There is no better place for the child to acquire and practice his mother-tongue than in his primary support group, the family. This acquisition starts long before formal schooling commences. Indeed, one can argue that the child will have ample opportunity to learn and practice English at school later. In contrast, the mother-tongue that fails to be presented to the child at home may never again be adequately presented to him all through his life.

The danger inherent in producing children who are not well grounded in their mother-tongue should not be underestimated. Such children grow up to be adults with dubious cultural identity. Worse still, such an adult will feel very uncomfortable conversing with his spouse in the mother-tongue, a situation which (as already explained) is a major predisposing factor pressuring the obliging family to slide towards English as the domestic language. The children growing up in such a family, in turn, will be poorly grounded in the mother-tongue; and so on. The attenuation of the mother-tongue in the home continues through succeeding generations, until the mother-tongue is completely lost, completely extinguished. Poor grounding in the mother-tongue is thus self-perpetuating through the generations of families, until we find that at the community level, a sizeable fraction of the ethnic group cannot even speak the language that identifies them. They are unable to show the prima facie identity card (language proficiency) to back up their claim to membership of the ethnic group. How can you convince me that you are Yoruba when you cannot speak Yoruba? Their claim to membership of the ethnic group can only be nominal and, in all sincerity, spurious.

For the mono-ethnic family living outside its indigenous linguistic area (but still within Nigeria), the child is sometimes faced with learning or using three languages at the same time: one for school (English), one for the street, and one for the home. For example, an Anioma child living in Calabar would have to juggle English in school, Efik on the street, and Anioma at home. Some families think that this is too much for the child, and justify using English at home so that the child only has to cope with two languages. This resolution to the problem underrates the considerable capacity of young children to learn several languages simultaneously, and to switch back and forth as the situation demands. Let us now examine why this solution must be considered facile.

The importance of the mother-tongue for the child is in no way diminished by his living outside his indigenous linguistic area. If anything, the mother-tongue in this case takes on added significance in at least two ways. First, the child living within his indigenous linguistic area has some opportunity to practice and use his mother-tongue on the street. In contrast, the child living outside his linguistic area is denied such an opportunity. His only meaningful contact with his mother-tongue must be within the home. If the mother-tongue is not available in the home, then it is not available at all. The need to offer the mother-tongue in the home is therefore more imperative here, even though paradoxically the pressure to install English as the domestic language is greater in this circumstance (as explained earlier).

Secondly, the child growing up outside his indigenous linguistic area is geographically distanced from and denied most of the cultural activities of his own people. The community cultural festivals, rituals, rites of passage, initiation rites, traditional ceremonies, etc. are usually performed within the geographical confines of his linguistic group, and are not readily available for such a child to participate in or observe. Unlike his counterpart who never left home, an Anioma child living in Lagos or New York is unable to observe the title-taking ceremonies, or new-yam festivals, or the bride-taking *ibu mmanya* that are a regular part of life within Anioma. By the sheer dictates of geography, he is denied many of the trappings of his indigenous culture. But there is one aspect of culture that can override the strictures of geography. That aspect is language. Language is, in a way, a portable aspect of culture. The child and his parents can indulge in it freely wherever they live, even outside the geographical confines of their indigenous linguistic area.

So, of all the facets of his native culture, the mother-tongue is perhaps the most readily available to the child living outside his indigenous linguistic area. If the child is now denied even this little aspect of his culture, then he grows up in a total cultural vacuum, since he is already denied most other aspects of his culture by sheer force of distance and geography. Just like fast food in the modern era, the mother-tongue is, therefore, a take-out slice of the indigenous culture, which the family can take wherever they go. Like the fast-food take-out, it may not offer all the ingredients for nourishment, but it can stave off cultural starvation and emaciation in the interim. The mother-tongue, then, is a slice of Anioma culture that is readily available to the Anioma child growing up in Lagos, Calabar, or Koton Karfi; or for that matter, in Chicago, Manila, Harare, Istanbul, or Santiago de Chile. No other slice of his culture is so globally accessible. No other slice is so globally portable. No child should be denied even this thin slice by parents who fail to present it.

For the family living outside its linguistic area, there is one additional, albeit peripheral, advantage to using the mother-tongue. The use of the mother-tongue by family members fosters a sense of belonging, cohesion, and exclusivity. The Anioma family in New York can carry on a spirited mother-tongue conversation in a public place without the risk of losing the confidentiality of their communication. It is as if they have access to a dedicated channel of communication that is not accessible to their neighbors. The family feels as one in their ability to use this channel. The ability to use the mother-tongue inspires in them much greater internal solidarity than if they could only communicate in the language used by everybody else around. Such a family also attracts a greater degree of authenticity to its claim that it has its origins in Anioma.

We see that for the mono-ethnic family, there is a strong temptation to have English as the domestic language when the family lives outside its indigenous linguistic area. Yet, it is precisely such a family that most desperately needs to have the mother-tongue as the domestic language. This is because the child has fewer casual opportunities to acquire the mother-tongue or to indulge in other aspects of his indigenous culture.

While the mono-ethnic family can maintain its mother-tongue as the domestic language by sheer will and unanimity, the situation is infinitely more complex for multi-ethnic families, where husband and wife hail from different linguistic groups. Such couples usually communicate with each other in English (or other lingua franca). The language question is either never addressed, or is allowed to take care of itself. In this situation, English offers itself least contentiously as the domestic lingua franca. Multi-ethnicity of the marriage is, therefore, a very strong pre-disposing factor for English to emerge as the domestic language. Culturally, the least commendable solution is the easiest to implement: the children grow up being proficient in English alone, and are unable to speak the language of either parent. This is like a dog-in-the-manger situation where each spouse, rather than concede to the other, prefers that neither of their mother-tongues should be the domestic language of the family. A more desirable option, for the sake of the children, could be for the family to adopt the language of one of the spouses as the domestic language. The actual choice of whose language should be adopted will be governed by the cultural expectations of the spouses, the language of the surrounding community, gender chauvinism, and whether one spouse already speaks the other spouse's language.

Then there is the very peculiar situation in which one of the spouses already has English (in any of its forms world-wide) as his or her mother-tongue. In that case, the choice is between introducing the language of the other spouse, or letting the family carry on with English as its only current domestic language.

Does it really matter if the Anioma family adopts English as its domestic language? Are there any disadvantages in adopting English, instead of the mother-tongue, as the domestic language? As already emphasized, the mother-tongue is of such crucial importance to a child's sense of identity and his world view that its acquisition should not be left to chance. A casual approach to the question by many individuals has already led to the use of English as the domestic language in an alarming number of families in Nigeria and globally. This has progressively led to the production of hordes of cultural eunuchs who, having long lost contact with their indigenous culture in deed, are now losing it in word as well. Worse still, such individuals tend to propagate the malady by generating mostly their own kind.

In the final analysis, everybody's circumstance is different. We also differ in terms of our degree of commitment to language preservation and propagation. Courtesy demands that we refrain from being judgmental about how each person or family has addressed this issue. However, there is something commendable about each family having a deliberate policy that permits the child to acquire and use his mother-tongue. The easiest way of achieving this is to entrench the mother-tongue as the domestic language for daily communication within the home. This is particularly important for the family sojourning in alien or foreign lands. In such cases, the mother-tongue serves as a portable and readily-available parcel of the home culture, while at the same time enhancing family cohesion and authenticity. The larger issue of preserving the communal/global cultural heritage also dictates that the mother-tongue should not be abandoned. The seeds of the global scourge of language extinction arise insidiously in the family that fails to pass on its language to its children. The mother-tongue is like the roof of your home in the Anioma proverb. If you do not mend and maintain the roof over your own home, who do you expect to do it for you? Nobody else will.

3

Straight Talk About Black Hair

Context: *Written in December 2002 in Chambersburg, Pennsylvania, USA. Updated in 2013.*

Nature has endowed humans with various kinds of hair texture, hair morphology, and hair color. For each race of humans, the hair characteristics are biologically determined. However, modern technology now enables individuals to alter their hair characteristics almost at will. But what happens when a race of people massively alter their hair to look like that of other races? What happens when a race of people conspires to turn its back on the kind of hair that is their natural inheritance?

Some pundits have remarked that many African Americans give the inescapable impression that they are somehow ashamed of the hair that nature gave them. Even if these remarks are misplaced, it is not difficult to see the evidence that has given rise to them. Could the supposed shame explain why, historically, the typical African American woman has gone to great lengths to straighten her hair or to attach unimaginable straight-hair pieces that enable her to copy the Caucasian ("white") hairstyles? There are other races (Chinese, Indians, etc.) around the world that have straight hair; but the historical impetus for African Americans straightening their hair came from the straight hair sported naturally by the white overlords. Straight "white" hair grew to be more acceptable than the curly hair of the blacks, who in turn did all they could to imitate the "white" hair.

Is it any wonder then that it's estimated that African American women in the US might "be 10% of the population but purchase 80% of the hair care products." Unfortunately, the classic stereotypical picture is one of a dirt-poor ghetto mother who can hardly feed her baby, but who spends much of her meager resources on the artificialities needed to keep her hair straight and "white". It is a picture of an inner-city ghetto neighborhood, devoid of decent grocery stores, but where the only flourishing businesses are hair and nail salons. The food deserts of the ghetto are luxuriant rain forests when it comes to hair care.

Indeed, in the most run-down black neighborhoods of America, the most prominent and prosperous businesses are usually hair and nail salons – all too ready to install their "natural" hair and nails on you, to replace the ones that nature gave you. The hair salon proprietors spare no effort to make you feel pity at how unkind nature was to give you such bad hair, and are ever ready to proffer their hair attachments as remedy for your misfortune. Food-stamp women, turning their backs on unpaid rents and unfed babies, routinely make regular pilgrimages to these salons to part with substantial proportions of their gross resources. Such is the lure of the straightened hair, the attached hair piece, and the stuck-on nails.

Unfortunately, this aping of white hair and white hairstyles has been allowed to infect black people all over the world, swept along, no doubt, by the global spread of American popular culture. Most of Africa is already infected. So is the Caribbean. It is only in places like Melanesia that you can still find most black women proudly wearing their curly hair in a non-white, un-straightened natural format. But even in such places, the inexorable march of the pattern set by African American women is already in evidence. Worse still, popular culture in America now seems to frown on black women wearing their hair naturally. How many times do we see "makeovers" on television, where a major part of the makeover is the straightening of curly hair on a black woman? They pejoratively call it "kinky hair" or "frizzy hair", something that nobody should want on their head. This gives rise to intense social pressures for young black women to conform, replacing their natural hair with "natural" attachments.

Virtually all the major role models for black women revel in and flaunt their straight "white" hair. Of the dozens of prominent black women actors and personalities, it is hard to name many that wear their hair in its non-white curly form. Even the ultimate role and fashion model, First Lady Michelle Obama, has been equally complicit in the straight-hair craze. Even though she wore her hair natural earlier in adulthood, the press successfully linked that hairstyle with rebellion and extremism. Consequently, she did not dare to wear the natural hair in her term as First Lady. Indeed, she sported a straight-hair look in her official portrait for Obama's first inauguration. Much to the dismay of many, her official look for the second inauguration saw her with an even straighter "whiter" hairstyle. As the press idolized her for the look, one could not escape the irony that it was all an artificial put-on. You could well have been complimenting her for what was, for all intents and purposes, a wig. The message to all the black women around the world was inescapable: the more you can straighten your hair, the better. In contrast, what a message it would have been to all black women if the First Lady wore her hair in anything close to its natural form even for a week; especially in her husband's second term when there were fewer political calculations to worry about. In the larger scheme of things, it was a huge opportunity missed when the First Lady failed to inspire authenticity among black women world-wide, and instead encouraged the borrowing of looks from some other ethnicity.

Because all their role models wear straightened hair, one must avoid being judgmental when we behold a black woman going around in "white" hair (many of my female relatives and friends are complicit). It is today's vogue and that's what society expects. But we should do all we can to assist black womenfolk to carve out and embrace an alternative paradigm that is consistent with the biology of their hair. Pride in their ethnicity would be considerably enhanced, not to mention a boost in their self-esteem. In addition, they could save the millions of dollars spent on frustratingly-repetitive straightening, applying sprays, and buying gaudy "attachments". Just as significant, they could avoid the risks posed to their health by the harsh hair chemicals, sprays, and ointments. With the current practice, their heads are constantly spinning in the suffusion of these applications, at great risk to life and limb and pocket.

During the black-consciousness era that accompanied the civil rights agitations of the 1960's, the wearing of black hair in an un-straightened fashion became the vogue. How could one forget the "Afro" hairdo of such icons of the era as Angela Davis and others? At that time, many rejoiced that black people had finally found their hair identity and had finally unyoked themselves from a damaged mentality that craved to look white. But the joy would not last. The almighty dollar was waiting to fight back. And it did with a vengeance. The hair products companies, who felt deprived of huge hair care profits, launched a vicious counterattack. Within five years, the Afro hairdo had become identified with sloppiness, and was in retreat. It has been in retreat ever since.

In recent years, some measure of African authenticity crept into the US black hair industry in the forms of plaiting and braiding. These have been the centuries-old methods of managing curly hair by black women in Africa. But these, especially braiding, are now so suffused with artificial hair ("attachments") that their authenticity is questionable. However, they have the redeeming feature of being uniquely identified with the African heritage.

Another recent hair trend, this time among African American men, has been to shave off all the head hair completely. The trend may have been boosted when people like Michael Jordan shaved their heads to accommodate early balding. It may be a passing fad, but the pace at which it has gained popularity lately has fed into the suspicion that black people disdain their natural hair. Let's not forget that only a couple of generations ago, it was commonplace for African American men to straighten their hair, a quirk that their womenfolk have retained to this day.

I would like to make a prediction. A time will come (maybe a century from now) when black people will look back with amazement at how much physical and financial effort black women spent to make their hair look like that of white people. By then, they would have weaned themselves from the ideology that the only good hair is one that looks straight and "white". They will look back and wonder what possessed them for so long. After all, if their menfolk could discard the habit, why not the women? Just like skin bleaching and hair straightening among men in an earlier generation, this egregious manifestation of a colonized mentality will also come to be a thing of the past. Right now, though, the "white" hair look is pervasive, and is even increasing in Africa and Melanesia where traditional "black" hairstyles have been the norm for centuries. The commercial purveyors of hair "straighteners" and attachments are winning the battle to maintain and expand the practice of blacks imitating the hair morphology of other ethnicities. These multinational hair-products companies are powerful, and will resist any effort by black women to wean themselves from the "white" hair products to which the women are currently addicted.

I'm eager to lend my voice to help trigger a hair care revolution that I have been expecting for years among blacks: one that embraces authenticity and rejects the expensive intrusion of chemicals, straighteners, and attachments. It is one that would promote black identity, while simultaneously reining in the strangulating strength of the black hair industry with its scalping sales practices.

Given the power of the hair care companies, it is not going to be easy to get black women to change their hair ways. It will require a concerted effort by prominent black men and women to effect this change. Are there people out there ready to sponsor significant competitions or promotions that truly manifest the beauty of natural black hair with a minimum of attachments and chemicals? Maybe some of the numerous black role models could take up the challenge, after they themselves have seen the light and can lead by example. It's time for heads to be held up high, naturally. It's time to stand up and be counted. It is time to step up to the plate. Who is ready to join the movement?

4

Is Murder More Socially Acceptable Than Sex?

Context: _Written on 16 December 2002, in Chambersburg, PA, USA._

Heavens forbid that we should be exposed to sex on family TV programs in America. Sex, even simulated sex, is clearly taboo on prime time family TV. You don't want kids watching simulated sex and getting ideas. You might see a couple kissing or fondling, but that's only as far as it can go. You don't see a simulation of the bumping and grinding of the sex act; not even scenes of a couple under the sheets doing the gyrating simulation. Such performances would immediately attract the opprobrium of the regulators of the airwaves. They would bar such a program or film from being shown to children or youth audiences. Family programs, we say, must be devoid of simulated sex acts.

Why do we not show such simulated sex images to young audiences? For most people, the apparent reason is that we simply do not want children to see simulated sex. Why? Because kids are impressionable and they might be tempted to practice what they see. So, we accept the premise that there is a link between what they watch and what they do or would be tempted to do.

If we accept this link, why then do we allow family programs to show simulated murder, simulated shootings, or simulated armed robbery? Indeed, many "family" programs cannot run for five minutes without one or more of such horrendous simulations. "But it's all simulated; none of it real," you may say. But the same argument could be applied to much of the sex that is withheld from non-adult view. If simulated sex can be seen as potentially damaging to non-adults, why are we in so much denial that simulated murder, shootings, and violence are also damaging to our children? In the pantheon of the detestable, is murder not just as abhorrent (or even more so) than precocious sex? Or, flipping the coin over, why should children be barred from watching simulated sex, when they are allowed free rein to watch simulations of murder, stabbings, and other heinous human manifestations? The way we are behaving, a visitor from outer space would conclude that murder (the simulation of which can be watched by everybody) is more acceptable to our society than sex (the simulation of which is for adult eyes only). How preposterous.

5

Bloody Good Sports: Catch-and-release fishing, and trophy hunting in perspective

__Context__: Written in July 2006 in Springfield, Missouri, USA.

The ancient Romans, with their gladiators and lion battles, took the art of blood sports to the limit. Hordes of ecstatic crowds routinely flocked to the Coliseum to watch the gore of humans battling beasts to the death. Great entertainment. Despite their highly civilized society, many Romans saw nothing wrong with shedding human blood and inflicting pain for entertainment. How far have we progressed since then?

Of course, blood sport the way it was practiced by the Romans would be considered barbaric today. But we still have overtly bloody sports like cockfighting, cage fighting, and bullfighting, where the drawing of blood and the infliction of pain is part of our entertainment. The gore in these sports is obvious, and much has been written about it. But what are some of the other more subtle blood sports that our civilized society tolerates, promotes, and even flaunts as urbane?

Let us look at hunting. In situations where hunting is done for food, the primary objective is not sport, even though stratagem, skill, and thrill in the kill are all involved. The main objectives are food procurement and human sustenance. These are worthy and existential goals that might outweigh the bloodiness of the exercise. However, in situations where the primary objectives are the leisurely pleasure of the hunt and the bagging of trophies, then hunting finds its place as a sport; a blood sport. Those indulging in this "sport" include the well-fed nobility in Europe galloping after foxes, the cash-paying millionaire trophy hunters tracking elephants in East Africa, and even the American adolescents sniping at jack rabbits for fun in their Midwestern backyard. The thrill of the kill is the primary motivation. Most of the animals are killed outright. So, to the extent that any blood sport can be considered humane, hunting is a humane blood sport. Unfortunately, many of the animals are maimed as they escape the hunt. They are doomed to misery for the rest of their lives, a fate for which the thrill-seeking hunter must bear some responsibility.

A slightly more insidious and invidious blood sport is found in catch-and-release fishing. On the face of it, this appears to reflect the apogee of the civilized human, since each fish that is caught has the hook removed from it and is mercifully thrown back into the water. The thrill in the "sport" is in catching the fish in the first place. But closer examination reveals a less glamorous picture. Each fish that is hooked suffers severe pain and bleeding right from the time it is hooked. The pain continues and the wounding is compounded as the fish is reeled in. More pain and wounding await the fish as the "sportsman" clumsily extricates the hook that has ploughed rampantly through the tissues of the fish. Even after the fish is thrown back into the water, the wounds probably continue to fester and must presumably lead to a miserable life thereafter. The question is: Is all this pain really necessary to assuage the sporting appetite of the angler?

Where fishing is done for food, then the pain is excusable for meeting the higher need of human sustenance. Even in such cases, the agony to the fish is less protracted since it is killed or dies shortly after it is reeled in. But for catch-and-release fishing, the agony is maximized. Not only does the wounded fish live on in protracted agony, but the purpose of the whole exercise is trivial and hedonistic. Pain to you, exclusively to promote my pleasure: that must be the ultimate definition of blood sporting. Does catch-and-release fishing really deserve its exalted place in our pantheon of civilized sports?

6

Pluralism In India:
Lessons for humanity

__Context__: Written in August 2006 in Springfield, Missouri, USA. It records thoughts that occurred at a certain time and place. The nature of this topic makes the time-frozen context important here.

The extent of pluralism and diversity in India is indeed breathtaking. Countries (like ours) that arrogantly claim to be the world's greatest bastion of democracy and diversity could do with a little humility, and learn a thing or two from the Indian experience. So, too, could most other countries with diverse ethnicities, nationalities, and religions.

For starters, India is the world's largest democracy, with more than a billion people in the mix. And what a mix it is! Because of the great diversity, the whole thing seems to be perpetually just about to tip over; always in a state of unstable equilibrium; always just below the boiling point; but still holding together and moving on. Communal riots, religious strife, devastating monsoon floods, low-level insurgencies, social/ caste stratification, and political assassinations are all part of the Indian experience. But somehow, the country stays together and marches on. Like a spinning top, the edifice manages to stay upright despite the whirling motion. The equilibrium is unstable, but it is an equilibrium no less.

We all know that the majority of Indians are Hindus. But even as I write this (in 2006), the President of India is not a Hindu, but a Muslim (Abdul Kalam). The Prime Minister of India is not a Hindu, but a Sikh (Singh). The Leader of the majority Congress party is not a Hindu, but a

Christian (Sonia Gandhi). And to Indians, there is no big deal in the fact that none of the three top positions in the country is occupied by someone from the majority Hindu group. Then there's a fact that very few people in the US realize: there are about as many Muslims in India as there are in its Muslim-identified archrival neighbor, Pakistan. Each one has nearly 180 million Muslims. Yes, as many Muslims in India as in Pakistan.

The vent that India gives to its pluralism is exemplified by the uniforms of its armed forces. It is interesting how the Sikh turban and beard have been co-opted to become part of the uniform for Sikh members of the armed forces. The turban and the beard are as much a part of the official uniform as the regular beret and clean shave. Then spare a thought for someone in the restaurant business in India, and the sheer diversity of clients with whom she has to cope. First, there is a sizeable proportion of the population who are vegetarians, up to 60% in the states of Gujarat and Rajasthan. A subset of these vegetarians would be the vegans who will not eat any animal products such as milk or eggs. Among the non-vegetarians (those that do eat meat), there are the Hindus who will not eat beef. Then there are the Muslims who will not eat pork. There are even sizeable numbers (such as some Jain devotees) who will not eat products that have been derived by killing a plant or animal. And finally, there is the residual population who will eat anything. Try putting together, on a daily basis, a restaurant menu docket that will cater to the varying requirements of this diverse clientele.

The pluralism of India is only matched by the role it has played in the recent history of mankind. India was the target that inspired many voyages of exploration over the past millennium, including the famous voyages by Columbus and Vasco da Gama. These were voyages which unwittingly opened up trade between Europe and various parts of the world besides India which was the intended destination. Eventually, India ended up giving its name to an ocean and to many regions of the earth such as the West Indies, East Indies, and Indo-China. By an accident of history, it also gave its name to the native peoples of the western hemisphere: American Indians, Amazon Indians, Pueblo Indians, etc. The name of India achieved a globality that could not be matched by even the great civilizations of Egypt, Greece, or Rome. No other nation, past or present, can lay claim to being such a pan-global marker.

. are run
urned to
ntriguing
ist party
iment in
ng these
sive edge
ave been
nitations
does not
sh in the
dom and
h-touted
depth of
at is not
?

the politics in India. While the US is still
:male head of government in over 230 years
igo, produced a female head of government
ii. This is something the US is yet to muster.
digress a bit, several supposedly anti-female
norter periods of existence, have also beaten
a female head of government. These include
(multiple times), and Indonesia. And so have
merica's hemisphere e.g. Brazil, Argentina,
Trinidad. The rooftop global champion of
s third century of all-male presidents. If the
imagine how much preaching, admonition,
have been dishing out to other countries to
r gender balance. In contrast, those who have
lly not tongue-lashed the US as they wait for
her cause for humility on our part; a reason
oris and the demonization of others in areas
ng behind.
y that exists in India, there is the matter of
n Indian politics. Just as in the US, there are
ir right of the spectrum. But then in India,
tend all the way to the left as well. For all its
eriously prohibits (even punishes) its citizens
iist party. And that means any communist
ied. Indeed, you cannot become naturalized
ver been a member of a communist party
paranoia, carefully nurtured with cold war
ne. But in India, the political space is wider.
s allowed communist parties to flourish and
laying field. In the process, the parties have
nitations. They will probably never win the
though they are part of the present ruling
hey have been allowed to contest elections
intry has not collapsed; fire and brimstone
ie skies. And in contesting, the communists
:d as governing majorities in some states. As

I write now, the state governments in Kerala and in West Ben
by the communist party, and the party has repeatedly been re
power in free and fair democratic elections. This is even more i
when you consider that for much of the time that the commu
was winning elections to control these states, the federal gover
New Delhi was controlled by the right-wing BJP party. In win
elections and running state governments, the presumed subve
has been taken out of the communists. More importantly, they
allowed to <u>show</u> what they are capable of doing and what their li
are, rather than our presuming or prejudging these factors. One
need to be an apologist for the left to say that letting them flou
political space in India is an infinitely greater manifestation of fre
democracy than the paranoid occlusion that occurs in our mu
"land of freedom." The world owes India (despite all its warts)
gratitude for this degree of tolerance, and for an experiment t
possible in most other "democratic" countries. Diversity, anyon

7

The Worm In The Big Apple

__Context__: A true story. Written 22 July, 2001, in New York, NY.

During the dog days of summer, I sought respite in, ironically, the city that never sleeps. New York City. The Big Apple.

It was July 2001. I had come from Pennsylvania to visit my son in New York City. On Sunday July 22, I decided to attend the church service at the Cathedral of St. John the Divine. After a long subway ride, I finally got off and started trudging up the hill towards the church. It was about 10 a.m. but the summer weather was already hot and steamy.

As I passed by a side street adjoining the church premises, I could see a human figure moving around in a cave-like cubicle underneath the church structures. Curiosity caused me to look closer. It was a woman; a black woman; apparently a homeless pauper who had all her bare belongings beside her in the cave. She was eating something that looked like a scanty sausage sandwich. Just as I was finally comprehending the situation, an equally bedraggled white male pauper showed up and approached her from the street. I paused to see what would happen. I thought she was going to run or scream. But no. Instead, she grabbed her sandwich, broke it in two, and offered one piece to the intruding fellow. He accepted thankfully, took a bite out of it, and was munching on it in no time. Both of them looked hungry, and from all appearances, neither of them could be satiated by a half-sandwich.

This pair had somehow managed to straddle the usual chasms between male and female, and between white and black in the city. Chasms that

41

their more affluent compatriots were having difficulty breaching. The one chasm that they had yet failed to straddle was that between the rich and the poor. I did not linger long enough to determine whether they had any prior or subsequent relationship. What was clear was that in the precincts of this magnificent cathedral, in the shadow of New York's lofty skyscrapers, an act of human love was playing out minutely among the lowliest in society. These kinds of people were, after all, the original targets of Christ's ministry. The woman who had virtually nothing was moved to share what little she had. It was only symbolically proper that they both should be clinging to the sheltering comfort of the church premises, however improvised it was. Watching this episode was more powerful than any churching or sermonizing that I would receive later that day.

While this little drama was playing out before my eyes, gigantic skyscrapers smiled down mockingly upon the scene, each building glittering in its summer elegance. Churchgoers in their Sunday best were pounding the sidewalks, heading for the church service with undistracted single-mindedness that precluded looking sideways. Big flashy cars were whizzing by, windows wound up to keep in their well-conditioned air. This odd couple was well beneath their notice, or their dignity. Like a film of flimsy gossamer, dodgyly discarded in a dank and dingy alleyway, the couple was not worth the gaze of those who may have found them useful earlier on. There was more reward in averting the gaze and focusing on the more pleasant, more affluent, surroundings. I looked up to contemplate all the gleaming skyscrapers around this destitute couple. The stench of opulence wafting in the air was suffocating. But somehow, it had eluded this pair. On that day and as usual, the Big Apple was impressively shiny on the outside. But the inside was something else. It definitely had a worm in it.

8

The Right To Rights: What of responsibilities?

Context: *First written on 16 August, 1997 in Lae, Papua New Guinea; then updated in 2006 in Springfield, Missouri, USA.*

I have a right to write this piece. And you have a right to read it. Or not. All over the world today, all kinds of "rights" are being asserted for people and by people. Old rights are being robustly protected, while new ones are being invented every day. They run the gamut alphabetically from "abortion rights" to "zoning rights" and more. Take your pick.

As we aggregate all these rights, the inevitable question is: Does every right have a concomitant *responsibility* attached to it? Should every right have a responsibility attached to it; or are there some innate rights that are bestowed, shorn of all responsibility? Should responsibilities that accompany each of these rights not be given equal consideration? While the answers may not be clear-cut, it seems that society would be better off if, at every point where rights are considered, the accompanying responsibilities (if any) are clearly articulated and understood.

The indiscriminate accumulation of rights by each individual, and the assertion of those rights, can only lead to societal friction, unless the responsibilities that go with those rights are exercised as well. Therefore, one of the responsibilities that should accompany each right is the judicious use of discretion in exercising the right.

In this regard, we can ask the question: Is there a distinction between rights that we *have* (claim) and rights that we *exercise*? I can claim to have a right to smoke in my bedroom, but do I still exercise that right if my spouse objects to bedroom smoking? For the good of the relationship, I sacrifice or suspend the exercise of that right. A responsibility that goes with my having the right is that I use discretion as to when and where I exercise that right. It is an example of where relationships are built on deference to each other; the voluntary refraining from exercising accepted rights, if such exercising will cause offense. It is the declaration of dependence and inter-dependence, a declaration which seems to lie at the very core of all loving relationships. It is this same declaration of dependence that lovers echo when they say, "I miss you," or, "I can't do without you," or even when they lean on each other as they walk along. Each one is willing, indeed eager, to thrust their vulnerabilities into the hands of the other for safe keeping, trusting that the vulnerabilities will be faithfully protected. Neither side expects the other to capitalize on the vulnerabilities.

So, a situation where everyone insists on exercising every right that they have, irrespective of the feelings of others, is a prescription for a chaotic, less amicable, mutual-avoidance, society. It is antithetical to peace. It is a harbinger of conflict and war.

A measure of how much you value a relationship is how many of your rights and comforts you are willing to "sacrifice" for the good of the relationship. I have a right not to take my child to his beloved soccer practice, not to attend my brother's wedding, etc. But each assertion of such rights makes a statement of how much or how little I value the relationship. For the good of the relationship and of society, I need to look in the compendium of rights that I have in my bag, and then carefully select which ones should rise to the level of being exercised. At any given time and for various reasons, most of my rights are latent and unexercised. Just resting in the bag.

When I decline to exercise certain rights, I do so out of robust respect for the rights of others and the feelings of others. Put differently, we are speaking of 3R's that go amicably together: Rights, Responsibilities, and Respect. The latter two are there to moderate the exercise of rights.

I wonder how all this plays into the current (2006) debate where European newspapers have not only used cartoons to caricature the prophet Mohammed (which goes against Islam), but have gone further to portray him as a ticking terrorist bomb. The right asserted here is the freedom of the press. It is an enshrined right in most western countries. But does the exercise of this right in this case show Muslims that you place any value on your relationship with them? Does it promote communal and global peace in a world where about a quarter of humanity are Muslims? Where is Respect, a factor whose primacy in non-western cultures is not fully appreciated by westerners?

Most newspapers in the United Kingdom (UK), for example, are very selective in exercising their freedom-of-press rights when it comes to publishing stories and pictures about the royal family. When compromising photographs of Prince Andrew partying in America came to light, most UK newspapers did not publish them. The same happened with photos of the Duchess of Cambridge sunbathing. The UK press refrained from asserting a right. They were willing to sacrifice or forego that right. Their doing so was a manifestation of the love and respect they have for the royal family. This made sense. A similar phenomenon exists in most western countries. Yet, those same papers were quick to assert their right and publish derogatory caricatures of the prophet, a double standard that went largely unacknowledged. Where were the love and respect for other humans? An indiscriminate assertion of rights is only compatible with an indiscriminate disregard of the feelings of others. This whole concept feeds into the idea that for every right ("freedom") there is a concomitant set of responsibilities. And the most fundamental of those responsibilities is the responsibility to discern when that right should be exercised.

Let's take a close look at two people: the cartoonist making caricatures of the prophet Mohammed, and the imam preaching virulent sermons that radicalize the youth. Both are provoking large segments of humanity against equally large segments of humanity; a taunting kind of provocation. The cartoonist claims to be exercising the cherished freedom of expression. Western society stridently backs up this claim. They encourage the cartoonist to carry on, holding his work aloft as a great example of how much their society values freedom of expression. This societal support makes the experience even more galling for all the people around the world who feel offended and violated by the cartoons. And western society is fully aware of this hurt. Is it not possible to celebrate free speech without promoting and patronizing its crassest expression? Some might even argue that serious damage is done to the cause of free expression when we continually thrust forward its most unsavory elements to be its flag bearer.

Now, let's talk about the virulent preacher. Could he also not claim to be exercising his freedom of expression? Is western society willing to protect the mantra of freedom of expression in this case? The experience is that, far from offering protection, western society is very keen to muzzle such expression, not only domestically but internationally as well. And such muzzling makes it obvious that our lofty free-speech proclamations to protect the cartoonist are all but empty hypocrisy. Numerous other examples abound where western society selectively and subjectively regulates the freedom of expression (try shouting "fire" in a crowded theater, or denying the holocaust in France). It is not that other societies are not equally culpable when it comes to free-speech rights. It's just that if you wear free speech as a signature badge, and haughtily castigate others for not wearing it, then you cannot but invite closer scrutiny.

There is a point at which free speech devolves into hate speech, a phenomenon that is indeed recognized as such in most societies. Hate speech is a weed that opportunistically infests the verdant cropland of free speech. It draws on the same nutrients as free speech and sometimes threatens to suffocate free speech. But while free speech yields bountiful bushels of grain, hate speech yields only barren burrs and thorny thistles. While free speech is a genuine coin in the realm of free expression, hate speech is a counterfeit facsimile which must not be allowed to contaminate the real thing.

So, even in western society, the holy grail of free expression is not inviolable after all. It is deceit and a disservice to the people for politicians to invoke the myth of unbridled absolute free speech as a veneer to give cover to contagious strains of anti-social behavior. There is much bluster in this posturing. So long as the west fails to rein in the likes of the cartoonist, so long will the likes of the virulent preacher continue to rail and assert their right to be heard. Both are asserting their right to free expression. But in my opinion, both the cartoonist and the preacher are equally guilty of not exercising that Right with a sense of Responsibility or a healthy Respect for other people. When it comes to both persons, a society that condones the one and condemns the other is guilty of crass hypocrisy. A society that celebrates the one and denigrates the other is exhibiting myopic arrogance. Both the cartoonist and the preacher should be condemned for insensitivity, and society should not be seen to be an apologist for either one.

Another current (2006) example illustrates the concept of responsibility in exercising rights. The crisis in the Anglican Communion about the ordination of gay bishops can be analyzed along similar lines. Of course, the US Anglican [Episcopal] church had the right to ordain gay bishops. All along, the Episcopal Church was fully aware that the rest of the global Anglican Communion was opposed to the practice. Little time and effort went into winning over the rest of the communion and building a consensus on the Episcopal position. So, when the US church went ahead and exercised the right anyway, it evoked the ire of the rest of the communion. The larger communion saw it as a statement of how little the US church valued its relationship with them. They, in response, were stung into devaluing their relationship with the US church. When I exercise my right to smoke in the bedroom, knowing fully well that my spouse is opposed to it, she is free to feel that I do not place a high value on her feelings or on our relationship. Similarly, when I exercise the right to stay away from my brother's wedding, he gets the clear message that I do not value our relationship. And just as with the Episcopal Church, there could be consequences.

We all have a right to rights; but we do not have a right to ignore the possible consequences of exercising those rights. It is our responsibility to exercise the rights with discretion and with respect for other people's feelings. The 3R's of Rights, Responsibility, and Respect, should always go together.

9

The Rung-Less Ladder From
The Economic Basement

Context: Written 22 September, 2004 in Chambersburg, Pennsylvania. I had gone shopping at the Salvation Army thrift store in Chambersburg.

Sometimes you need a minor incident to jolt you into contemplation of bigger issues. I've just come back from the Salvation Army thrift store where I went for my usual bargains in used clothing. It was a habit I had formed because it represented a confluence of three precepts that were dear to me: frugality, philanthropy, and sustainability through recycling.

While at the shop, I finally settled on a pair of decent brown shoes for less than two dollars. I stepped up to the customer line in front of the checkout counter. The woman just ahead of me in the line was a fortyish white woman, with graying hair. She was having difficulty with the choices of clothing she had brought forward. She looked confused and harried in her indecisiveness. So, the counter clerk asked her to step aside so I could be served. After I had paid $1.69 for my shoes, the woman was asked again if she was ready. She was not. She was still immersed in her choice conflicts, and passively muttered, "...I don't have enough money...," suggesting that her preferred item was beyond what she could immediately afford. This meant that she would either have to forego it, or settle for a less preferred item. The lowest rung of the economic ladder was missing. In vain she struggled to get a footing where the rung should have been.

While the customer woman's indecision lasted, the person behind me in the line moved forward to be served. I left the shop. After thinking for a moment about what had just happened, I returned to the shop. I thrust a twenty-dollar note into the woman's hand. She resisted strongly, but on my insistence, she finally took the money. The old counter clerk lady, who had seen me penny-pinching at that shop many times before, was looking on in amazement.

My analysis of the situation is that if this had happened at an up-scale shop, I probably would not have helped out. But this woman had come down to the basement of the consumer ladder (used clothing) and was still having financial difficulty. Even if she was buying more than she needed, she deserved any help that was available. Despite her apparent poverty, her initial strident resistance to my offer was a gallant stance in defense of her self-respect. The poverty that had fretted her purse had not reached into her inner being. It is amazing that I, who was angling for the last penny of the deepest discount possible on my purchase, was so willing to part with the twenty-dollar bill. Yes, this was for a more existential purpose. I just barely needed those brown shoes, and they had to be cheap enough to tempt me to buy them. This woman, in contrast, probably needed every bit of what she was trying to buy.

At the sociological level, I was asking myself: Is it possible that this white woman customer had never received an act of kindness from a black person, and may not even have ever interacted with one? A similar question could be asked of the white lady clerk, looking on in amazement. Such is the poverty matrix in America. It knows no racial boundaries.

10

Diversity And *Change:* Exemplified in agricultural, economic, and political systems

__Context__: Written between 18 July, 1997 and 28 October 2000, in Lae, Papua New Guinea.

We all talk about *diversity*. What does it really mean? In America today, the word immediately evokes the concept of racial diversity, and the myriads of related social phenomena. But how prevalent and important is diversity outside the racial context? Can it be found in the agricultural, economic, and political realms, and how useful is it in those circumstances?

What would happen if there was no *competition* between organisms in the biological realm? In such a situation, there would be no evolution. The theory of evolution is based on competition in which the fittest survive to continue the line, while the weakest are annihilated. Just as evolution depends on competition, so does competition depend on the fact that there is variability (diversity) within the population. Without this diversity, there would be no evolutionary progress; i.e. if all individuals are the same, either all survive or all perish in the face of change in the ambient environment. Indeed, diversity is a stabilizing factor for the system, since it gives it a way out when the prevailing conditions change.

Just as in biological systems, I believe that this concept of evolution through diversity is applicable to many other aspects of human existence. Take agriculture for example. A country which fails to diversify its food sources, and allows itself to become dependent on a narrow range of commodities, is only living in an unstable equilibrium. In the 19th century, Ireland allowed itself to become almost solely dependent on the potato as its food crop. There was little diversity. This was okay as long as the prevailing environment remained steady and did not change. But the environment changed. When the potato blight *(Phytophthora)* struck and created a new environmental circumstance, it really struck devastatingly. There was nothing to fall back on, and the Irish were reduced to ruins. A good proportion of them had to flee the country, and thank goodness, there was America to migrate to. If the food basket had been diversified, the impact of the calamity would have been much less. More recently, in the last decade of the 20th century, a similar thing has happened in Samoa. The food system of affluent subsistence was not diversified. It relied disproportionately on taro. Again, things went on swimmingly for decades, until the taro leaf blight struck in 1993. The food economy, resting on one leg, was devastated. The United Nations had to rush in experts (including yours truly) to try to tackle the problem. Even as I write now (1997), the country is still reeling from the punch, and is only belatedly scrambling to diversify its food basket. Other more or less dramatic examples of the need for diversity in food/agriculture can be found around the world.

Still on agriculture, the need for diversity also implies that various corners of the world should be encouraged to continue to grow foods, crops, and livestock which are unique to them, but which the rest of the world may consider obscure, useless, or uneconomical for now. The recent global interest in land races and heirloom varieties of crops is a welcome nod in this direction. The day may come when the predominant commodities/varieties are devastated, and the world's lifeline will be a long-neglected obscure crop. The present tendency to homogenize the world's food diet in favor of just a few commodities should be considered an unsavory development.

The importance of biodiversity in the world's forests is very well known and well publicized. It needs little elaboration here.

If diversity is important in the biological sciences, it is also just as important and relevant in the social sciences, especially economics and politics. One important aspect of diversity in economics is that the offering of a diverse array of products/services permits competition and the survival of the best product. So much of capitalist economic theory is based on this concept. Capitalism depends on competition which depends on diversity of products.

Taking the point one step further, I believe that the benefits of diversity in economics go beyond the diversity of products/services. Diversity of economic *systems* should also be beneficial. Conversely, a failure to diversify the world's economic systems will be harmful in the long run. The undiversified system becomes moribund, self-conceited, and eventually decays from within in its self-assumed perfection. The present push to get the whole world to adopt the capitalist system should be seen in this light. Good as it may be, capitalism has many shortcomings. Other systems should be permitted, indeed encouraged, to compete with capitalism to proffer solutions where they can (while exposing their own shortcomings). This, after all, is a higher level of competition and survival.

It is strange that some of the strongest proponents of competition within capitalism are the greatest opponents to evolving other systems that can compete with capitalism. This is harmful enough. But perhaps more pernicious is the arrogance with which capitalism is being peddled as the ultimate in human perfection, and therefore not in need of any improvements or reform. All other systems are bullied and bludgeoned into reforming towards it (capitalism), while it assumes the mantle of perfection and resists reform (witness Hillary Clinton's efforts to reform the capitalist-modeled US health care system during her husband's administration. The effort failed).

In politics too, diversity and competition are essential. It is the diversity of political parties/candidates, with competition between them, that enables the electorate to choose, and lets the system produce the best outcome. But can we not carry this concept of diversity-with-competition to political *systems* as well? Indeed, it is desirable that at any given time, the world should be "experimenting" with several political systems. So again, all the bullying and shouting, trying to get the whole world to adopt "western democracy", may ultimately prove to be counter-productive. The present peddlers of capitalism and "western democracy" as the ultimate solution to the human condition, could well do with a little humility. They should realize that unless their "perfect" system is ready to tolerate diversity, competition, reform, and evolution, it too will fail in the long run.

This same principle of diversity is also applicable to the cultures and religions of human societies. The global colonial enterprise of the past half-millennium has stridently sought to replace the culture and religion of the colonized with that of the colonizers. Sometimes, the intent has been good; but it betrays a haughty lack of respect for the cultures and religions of the indigenous peoples. The colonizer is so certain of the veracity of his cultural/religious package that he brooks no possible competing packages. This brazen lack of humility, with the accompanying hegemonic effort to obliterate diversity, has led to unpleasant consequences in various parts of the world.

Very closely related to diversity is the concept of *change*. Change is akin to biological mutation, the engine that drives evolution forward. Even though most biological mutations are deleterious, nature still indulges in producing myriads of them. The benefits of the few good ones make it all worthwhile. So it is with change. Most changes, especially those not brought on deliberately, may turn out to be harmful. But the resilience of the system lies in its diversity which ultimately enables it to adapt. In biological systems, mutations give rise to diversity which is so critical for evolutionary progress through competitive selection. Similarly, it is change that produces diversity in political and social systems. What mutation is to biological systems, change is to political/social systems. Political/social *evolutionary progress* depends on *competition* which depends on *diversity* which depends on *change*. Said differently, change produces diversity which permits the competition that will result in evolutionary progress. It is change that sets the entire train in motion. Without it, the train is stuck at the station.

Important as it is, change is often most effective when administered in frequent small doses. Sudden large doses tend to be catastrophic. At the sociological, political, or economic levels, small changes that are made, monitored, and subjected to further changes, make the big cataclysmic change unnecessary. The system evolves gradually without resorting to convulsion. It is only when evolution has been stifled that Revolution becomes necessary. We should remember that the sculpture masterpiece does not result from one big hammer blow (the big change); it results from a series of small subtle blows (small changes) delivered over time.

11

Egalitarian Humanism

Context: _Written on 9 July, 2003 in Chambersburg, PA, USA._

W hat do you call a philosophy that recognizes that all persons have their humanity as the one common and equalizing denominator? I give it the name: _Egalitarian Humanism_. It is a philosophy that has arisen _sui generis_ from my contemplations, and it may or may not resemble the philosophy that has been espoused by any other person.

For any person, when you remove all the trappings and pretentiousness; remove all the titles and "bestowments"; remove all the riches and adornments; remove all the penury and poverty; remove all the infirmities and inadequacies; what do you have left? The irremovable and inalienable core that you have left is the human being – deserving of a certain quantum of dignity at the minimum, but equally susceptible to foibles. Just as the most exalted person is subject to human frailty, so it is that the lowliest person is deserving of human dignity. When big-time politicians and religious leaders yield to sexual or financial indiscretions, we are surprised. But we should not be. They are simply manifesting the frailties that derive from their being human. Exalted as they are, it is impossible for them to escape from the orbit of being human. Similarly, most modern societies insist that the poorest, sickest, and weakest members of society have a right to life and to a political vote equal to that of the richest person in the society. The lowly cannot drop below the minimum level of dignity/ recognition that derives from their being human. Our humanity is like the midpoint of a pendulum which, though it can swing to either side, will always tend to return to the middle.

Egalitarian humanism tends to chip away at the edges and extremes of the human condition, tending always to push the poor, the rich, the sad, the euphoric, the healthy, the sick, the strong, the weak – all of them towards the middle ground of their basic human condition. In other words, being human sets upper and lower limits beyond which nobody can range. The noble still remain burdened with frailties; those of humble estate still have a minimum level of inalienable dignity. Just as no one is beyond corruption, so also no one is beyond redemption. That is my idea of Egalitarian Humanism. Remember that before anything else, besides everything, on top of everything, and if nothing else, YOU ARE HUMAN.

12

Self-Serving Munificence,
And Pet Peeves

Context: _Written on 8 June, 2006 in Springfield, Missouri, USA._

What is the nature of the relationship that exists between the beef rancher (herd owner) and the cattle? Here's what the cattle said to the rancher...

"You feed me when I'm hungry; and even when I'm not.
Without you, I would probably go hungry and get skinny.
You protect me from the elements and nurse me when I'm sick.
Without you, I would have died of sickness in my youth.
My life has been a bed of roses because of your care...
But now in my adulthood, I feel thorns poking through the roses.
Just when I felt that all your loving care was indeed loving,
I hear that you are negotiating with the manager of the slaughterhouse.
You want to pass me on to him to meet my fate as meat.
Have you been good to me all along only because it serves your purpose,
Knowing that your ultimate design has been to get me killed?"

The rancher had no answer. This kind of asymmetrical relationship also occurs in many other spheres of life. A master feeds the slave plenty of food so that the slave can have enough strength to do work for the master. The predatory lender supports the debtor so that the debtor will be able to continue repaying the compounded loan for as long as possible. He wants the debtor to survive enough to continue repaying, but not to thrive enough to pay off the loan. International creditors that lend to poor countries seem to have a similar strategy with respect to their debtor countries. Foreign aid is carefully titrated in such a way as to perpetuate dependency: enough for the recipient to keep going, but not enough to make them prosper beyond needing foreign aid in perpetuity. Similarly, even neo-colonial powers will keep their client states supported enough that they do not buckle under, but not allow them to mature to the extent that they revolt against their client-state status.

All this is similar to the relationship between many pet owners and their pets. The cost to the pet of being loved is that it has to be castrated (spayed/neutered). In doing this, the owners feel a sense of moral superiority that they are preventing unwanted litters. But do they consider for a moment that they are depriving the pet animal of a meaningful sex life for life? How would the owners or their children like to live a sexless life as a price for being loved? And by the way, when we say, "unwanted litters," we may ask, unwanted by whom? Unwanted by the owner and his species, but not unwanted by the pet species. Biologically, virtually all species love to procreate, and love their offspring. Pet species are no exception. Who gave the owner the moral right for population control among the pet species? Instead of this highly conditional love, would the pet species have preferred a full sex life and the ability to procreate? Just like feeding/loving and then killing the cow, castration is a manifestation of exploitation in an asymmetrical relationship. It may be a pragmatic necessity, but it should never be held up as a holier-than-thou flag to be waved from a moral high ground.

Outside the realm of human activity, self-serving munificence is very common in nature. The parasite that immediately kills its host deprives itself of its own basis of survival. The most successful parasites and predators are those that somehow pamper the host, at least for a while. They let the host thrive while (or before) they figuratively suck it dry. So the rancher, the predatory lender, the neo-colonialist, and the pet owner have definite counterparts in nature. Go figure.

13

Love = Affection + Devotion: Should it be inclusive or exclusive?

> **_Context_**: *These ideas were first developed on 8 October 1997 and updated 29 August 2000, both in Papua New Guinea; further embellished in June 2013 in Maryland, USA. The definition of love indicated here has arisen from my own musings; it may or may not align with what others have thought.*

What exactly do we mean by love? When an adolescent man beholds a beautiful girl, he is attracted to her. This, I would like to call *affection*. This attraction occurs even if neither the girl nor the man has done anything to bring it about or foster it. In that sense, it is a passive interaction. The young man is free to leave it at that and go his own way. We cannot declare that he has fallen in love with the girl. However, as often happens, he may decide to do something about the attraction. He embarks on an active set of deeds to promote, enhance, and foster their mutual attraction to each other. He improves his physical presentation, offers gifts, provides entertainment, etc. This set of active moves I would refer to as *devotion* to the girl. While affection is relatively passive, devotion involves an active set of maneuvers, by the man and/or the girl. It is when affection is followed up by devotion that we can say that the boy is in *love* with the girl. While there may be other ingredients involved in love, it seems that, put succinctly:

Affection + Devotion => Love

Affection that is not followed up by devotion remains just that. Conversely, devotion that is not accompanied by affection is not truly love, as can be seen in situations of serfdom, or in some arranged marriages.

Even in non-romantic contexts, these two ingredients appear to be essential for us to say that true love exists. The parents have affection for their child. But they do not stop there. They constantly act out devotion in the form of taking care of the child's physical and emotional needs. It is the devotion that enables the bonds of affection to grow. Their affection followed up with devotion is tantamount to love.

Love is one of the most abused words in the modern human lexicon. It is bandied around lightly, even in situations where incipient hatred is obvious. One of the more contentious aspects of love is whether it should be exclusive or inclusive. Let us examine this aspect briefly.

In spiritual circles, the love of God, from which all else is supposedly derived, is inclusive rather exclusive. We conceive of it as embracing everyone and everything. We also see it as being enduring; having staying power well beyond human propensity to reject it through wrongdoing. Why then should our own love be exclusive? Genuine human love, it seems, must be inclusive and constantly seek to expand its coverage. It should be able to embrace mother, father, sisters, daughters, brothers, wife, husband, neighbors. In addition to current spouse or lover, it could also embrace ex-spouses and ex-lovers. Just as God loves us all at the same time, yes, you can love several people at the same time, sharing both affection and devotion with each of them. What perhaps could be exclusive is *sex*. Rising above our raw biological instincts, human civilizations have developed institutions that make sex exclusive to one partner (or a small group of partners in polygamous societies) at any given time.

Moralists will always ask a man, "How can you say you love Ms. X when you're still in love with Ms. Y?" Television shows and the mass media are full of such questioning. It is almost as if loving one person forces you to de-love the other person; like a zero-sum game where one person's gain must be another person's loss. Indeed, if the love of the first person was genuine to begin with, it should not be so evanescent, so easily effaced in the face of a new object of love. The inclusive nature of love comes into play here. The honest answer to the question is that it is perfectly possible to love both persons, and this happens frequently. When moralists espouse that you can only love one person at a time, they are probably talking about having one sexual partner at a time, rather than actually loving only one person at a time. Indeed, you should be able to love many people simultaneously, including non-relatives of either gender who do not automatically become potential sexual partners. Conversely, it should be possible for you to remain in love with somebody who has ceased to be a sexual partner; just as you can love someone who has never been and will never be a sexual partner. It sounds nice and glib to say that you can only love one person at a time; but reality gives a lie to that construct. Perhaps a clearer separation and definition of love and sex might be beneficial to society.

14

Conversation With A Grain Of Rice

Context: *Written in 2014 in Maryland, USA.*

In the summer of 2007, I was invited for dinner at the home of a colleague. Part of the menu consisted of rice and stir-fry. I took my seat at the dinner table, while my host and his wife were dishing up and scurrying around. Shortly, his wife came around with my plate of rice and placed it in front of me, before quickly disappearing again into the kitchen. As she plopped the plate of rice down on the table, one grain of rice fell from the plate onto the table. I looked intently at the grain of rice. I contemplated how far it had come to reach my dinner plate, only to be bumped off at the last minute. As I fixed my gaze on that grain of rice, I began to contemplate the tale that it could have had to tell me, and the lessons therefrom…

I was born in the swampy lands beside the Chao Phraya River in Thailand. Not really born in the sense of being pushed out of a womb, but more in the sense of coming into existence through a fertilization process. My destiny in life was to feed humans. It was my main purpose for existing, and a role that I was very eager to fulfill.

My father was borne in the wind, one of millions of potential pollen fathers that could have alighted on my mother. Within weeks of my parents meeting, I was already a soft squishy milky blob, tightly wrapped within my mother. Despite the cocoon-like wrappings, it was still a precarious existence because insects and diseases devastated some of my neighbors. But I was lucky to escape the ravages of all the pestilence. I got harder as time went on, and by the time I was two months old, I was a well-hardened kernel, still tightly wrapped in my brown husk. I was getting harder by the day as I lost the excess moisture. Then one day, the owner of our farm came with his sickle. He detached our stalk from our parent plant, allowing hardly any time for me to say goodbye to my mother. He bundled the stalks together and carried us to a courtyard near his house. There he laid us out in the sun each day to dry out some more. Through my husk, I could spy rats and mice that paid visits to us each night. They consumed some of my neighbors, but again, I was lucky to escape being devoured by them.

Early on one sunny day, the farmer and his wife bundled us into a sack and took us to a rice mill. There they said goodbye to us, having received some payment from the miller for bringing us there. I felt sorry to see the farmer go, but I had no choice or voice in the matter. Having been brusquely separated from my mother earlier, I was now being abandoned by the farmer who had nourished us while we were in the field.

The miller dumped us, still in the sack, with hundreds of other sacks that were in his shed. We lay there for about a week, with drafts of warm dry air bathing us all the time. Then it was time for our denudation. As all kinds of machines whirled and roared, we were shuttled through various tight spaces whose main purpose seemed to be to remove the protective husk that covered each of us. It seems that some of my mates had been parboiled before this denudation procedure, but I and other members of my sack escaped the boiling process.

Next, they put us through some other machines with abrasive parts that progressively removed the brown outer covering from our now-naked bodies. This step was particularly hurtful to me. Not only was it extremely painful, but it also caused me to lose most of my vitamins. I lost my golden tan and was now albino-white.

By this time, my original sack-mates and I had lost contact with one another. We had been mixed in with grains from hundreds of other sacks, and re-bagged into smaller 20-pound bags. I had new bag-mates. Next, we were taken to a large warehouse at the district headquarters. We stayed there for about three weeks, and were then moved to Khlong Toei, the port of Bangkok. Rumor had it that we were about to embark on a long voyage.

Just as suspected, after a week at the port, we were loaded into the bowels of a big cargo ship. Once the ship set sail, we began to feel the rolling and rocking motion as it battled the heavy seas. The rocking and rolling motion continued intermittently for about a month. Then one day, the door of the ship's hold where we were kept swung open. Soon, they began to take us out to deliver us to dry land. From all indications, this was now a new country. We were now in America, at the port of Long Beach, California. After weeks of incarceration in the dark holds of the ship, this looked like progress. Soon we were loaded onto a train that was to take us to the heart of America.

Our train traveled fast, but had two long layovers before we eventually reached Chicago. In Chicago, we were loaded onto huge trucks for a further leg of our journey. Once loaded, the journey took less than a day. We were off-loaded in Springfield, Missouri, and shoved unceremoniously into a warehouse. We sat there in the winter cold for about three weeks. Then the bag I was in got loaded onto a truck that belonged to a store specializing in oriental groceries. The store owner offloaded us as soon as he got to his store. Within days, we were already being displayed in the store as newly-arrived rice from Thailand. Some bags were picked up by customers within days; but the bag containing me and others stayed there on the shelf for weeks. I was beginning to wonder if I would ever be able to fulfill my destiny of serving as food for a human.

Eventually, a professor at one of the local universities picked up my bag. He took us home, but then again the wait continued. Shelf time at the grocery store had simply been replaced by shelf time in the professor's pantry. One Wednesday night, he eventually opened up the bag that contained me and others. He scooped out some of us, but I was not one of the lucky ones. He closed the bag, and my wait in the pantry continued. A little over two weeks later, his wife came to the pantry. As she struggled to open the bag, some of my bag-mates fell on the floor and were later swept up and discarded. Their destiny was the dustbin, contrary to their desired destiny of feeding a human. Fortunately, I was not one of those discarded. Using a measuring cup, the lady eventually took out a couple of scoops of rice. I was lucky to be one of the grains scooped up. She washed us in water, placed us in her rice cooker, and the steaming began. In 15 minutes, I was nice, white, plump, and ready to nourish a human being. We stayed in the rice cooker until their dinner guest arrived. I was part of a large spoonful placed on the plate for the dinner guest, although I found myself precariously at the edge of the plate. Just as the hostess placed the plate in front of the guest, the plate bumped the table and I was knocked out of my perch. I landed on the tablecloth, a few inches beside the plate. I looked at the guest and he looked at me. What was he going to do?

Is this guest more concerned about the hygiene of the tablecloth than about my current plight? Will he pick me up and put me back on the plate with the other grains, or even pop me into his mouth ahead of the other grains? After my long journey from the swamps of Thailand, through pestilence, complex machinery, heavy seas, and multiple spillages, am I now going to fall by the wayside and fail to nourish a human? Or is the guest, out of consideration for how far I have come, going to pick me up and nourish himself with me? Will this be a fateful twist on the classic case of a slip twixt the tongue and the lip? My journey has been long and tedious. It would be a shame for it to be aborted at this final stage.

Even if the guest does not pick me up, I'm sure that the next time he decides to throw away an item of food, he will pause a bit. He will spare a thought for the tortuous route that the item has taken to reach his table, and all the factors that could have prevented it from arriving there. Each particle of food that manages to reach the dining table represents a victory, and should be celebrated as such.

…With all these thoughts to consider, what would you have done with this grain of rice?

15

The Agnostic's Prayer

Context: *Written on 13 April, 1999, in Lae, Papua New Guinea. Edited in 2014.*

What percentage of the cosmos can humans really claim to know? It is certain that what we know of the universe is only a very small fraction of the entire thing. What we do not know is so much bigger, so much greater, than what we know. What we already know is extremely complex; so the mind must boggle at the potential complexity of the larger part which we do not know, and which we may never have a way of knowing.

The more we know, the more we know how little we know. Based on the infinitesimal fraction which we know, the universe is extremely ordered even in its complexity. Yet could all this complexity be random or could it be self-ordering? Alternatively, and in the absence of any ability to gain an insight, could we logically presume that all the complexity (known and potential) and order in the universe must have a force or source for its genesis and regulation? For the purposes of this discussion, we can simply refer to this regulating manifestation as Z, resembling but not identical with what has led many religionists to the various concepts of God over the ages.

Judging by the infinite magnitude and complexity of the domain which Z controls, Z must presumably be endowed with infinite powers. Because we only know a very small fraction of the universe, we can only know a very small fraction of the powers of Z. A full comprehension of the powers of Z is well beyond humans now, and possibly for ever.

The agnostic in me says that Z is so huge, so complex, so everything, that I am a totally insignificant component in the large universe which Z controls. A case for insignificance can also be made for human beings as a group, and even for the entire planet Earth. Photographs of Earth taken by the Voyager spacecraft from the edge of the solar system dramatically emphasize that our blue planet is but a speck of dust in a vast, incomprehensible, unfathomable desert. A desert with similar specks of dust perched around zillions of sand grains, each grain representing a star heavenly body. How on earth could our dust speck be the center of this mind-boggling vastness? Our gigantic Earth never felt so small. We, its inhabitants, could only marvel at our new-found obscurity. Not since Copernicus and Galileo has our sense of centrality in the universe been so significantly downgraded. And the downgrading is likely to continue as our megalomania takes a pounding with each scientific discovery.

Consider for a moment a single bacterium merrily living out its life inside a single cell in my small intestine. This bacterium, lodged close to the cell nucleus, is unable to comprehend the totality of that cell. Even if it had a means of sending probes to the mitochondria on the other side of the cell, it would consider it quite an achievement in its exploration. How could that bacterium comprehend the existence of the totality of my gut, of me, of my city, of the Earth, of the solar system, of our Milky Way galaxy, etc.? Impossible! As far as that bacterium is concerned, the universe consists of the entanglements of its host cell, and perhaps slightly beyond. It has no means or capacity to fathom the great expanse that lies outside. Could the existence of this bacterium relative to the solar system be analogous to the existence of human beings relative to the universe: something to which we can have no clue, however hard we try and however much exploration we think we have accomplished?

If we are so insignificant before Z and all that it influences, is it possible for Z to control what we humans do? The answer seems to be yes, given the all-powerful nature of Z. This specific characteristic enables it to control and direct even the minutest detail of the universe and of our existence in it. Even the electrons swirling around the nucleus of an atom are directly or indirectly under the control of Z or laws laid down by Z. I say "indirectly" because science can sometimes offer an immediate explanation, then an explanation of the first explanation, and so on. But, ultimately, there is a residue that is totally unexplainable and is simply ascribed as the innate characteristic or property of the item in question. How are those innate properties bestowed? This is where Z comes in.

If we are so insignificant before Z, is it possible for us to influence what Z does? I think not, given the impotence that derives from our insignificance. But then, this immediately raises the question of what we hope to achieve by praying to Z. Is prayer a totally futile exercise, trying to extend our reach towards the unreachable? It seems that Z can reach us when Z wants to, but I fear that the reverse is probably not true. We cannot reach Z when we want to. But Z can condescend to reach us in response to our wanting to reach Z.

Let us take the prayer that is in the form of praise and thanksgiving. Does Z really need our praise or even our thanksgiving? Our praise may be significant to us, but it's probably totally insignificant before Z. Z suffers no diminution in the absence of our praise or thanksgiving. Z can well do without them. So the prayer of praise/thanksgiving serves the purpose of making us feel good. It is us that need it, not Z that needs it. The same could be said of the prayer of supplication. If our intention is to intervene and change the will of Z, then our exercise may be totally futile. Unless of course Z is pleased to reach down and reward us for our effort. We cannot reach up, but Z can reach down, figuratively speaking.

It seems then that in prayer, we are reacting in human terms, to a benefactor that is not human. We show gratitude, we praise, we supplicate, just as we would do to a human benefactor. Being human, we know no other way to respond to a benefactor. Since Z understands our human limitation, Z could decide to acknowledge our effort and sincerity, and then to reward us for both. So, even though Z does not need the praise, thanksgiving etc., Z is able to understand why we do it, to take note of them, and to reward us for the sincere effort that we put in. In this context, then, prayer may not be totally useless. It is an indication of our vain effort to reach Z. Apart from making us feel good, it might result in some reward from Z for the sincerity of our effort.

16

Religion And National
Cultural Identity

*__Context__: Written in Lae, Papua New Guinea on 26
June, 1997.*

Is it possible to separate language from cultural identity? Can you strip
away the language associated with a culture and still have a vibrant
culture? The answer is almost certainly no. "Culture" seems to be one
giant jigsaw puzzle of which language is one indispensable piece. Remove
the language and you leave a gaping hole. A culture that is shorn of its
associated language is but a motionless skeleton devoid of the flesh muscle
needed to motivate it. Culture and language appear to be inextricably
linked.

But what about separating religion from cultural identity? Can it be
done? The answer is not so clear. Religion seems to be another piece of
the same culture jigsaw puzzle. The indigenous religion of a people would
have evolved in intricate relationship with the culture. There is a definite
limit on the ability to remove one piece of the jigsaw from the "religion"
position and then substitute a different "religion" piece within the same
cultural jigsaw landscape. As with real jigsaw puzzles, the substitute piece
is unlikely to fit perfectly. This is what often happens when a religion is
transplanted from one culture where it has developed, across to an alien
culture.

It is not surprising therefore, that religious and cultural boundaries
tend to coincide. In many cases, the cultural boundaries are the same

as national (with small "n"; same as ethnic group) boundaries, and each nation tends to evolve its own religion or brand of existing religion.

What happens when a religion is transplanted from its cultural origin to an alien culture? It tends to come under severe stress, and is invariably modified to fit the "religion" space in the new cultural jig-saw. Take Christianity for example. Apart from the initial modifications from its Jewish roots, it has so far evolved into numerous ethnic-specific churches: Greek orthodox, Russian orthodox, Serbian orthodox, Church of England, Dutch Reformed Church, etc.; not to mention the numerous ethnically modified versions of Christianity that exist in Africa, Mayan America, and many other parts of the world. Similarly, Buddhism underwent significant modifications as it migrated from its birthplace in northern India to the cultures of China and the Far East. Most of these changes were attempts to modify the imported religion to fit the local cultural jigsaw space.

Given the close relationship between religion and the ethnic unit, it is not surprising that over the ages, there has been a strong tendency to combine religious rulership with national rulership. God-kings abound throughout history, from ancient Egypt to modern-day Himalayan entities. Again turning to Christianity, the early popes wielded both spiritual and temporal supremacy over the people. Many medieval rulers in Europe asserted the divine right of kings. As Christianity spread, various other nations also tried to maneuver so that their temporal heads could become their spiritual heads as well. When King Henry VIII assumed the titular headship of the Church of England, he achieved two things at once: he amalgamated the temporal and religious headship into one person; and he in effect "nationalized" the religion which was now supposed to be remolded to fit the "religion" position of the jigsaw of English culture. These two "achievements" of King Henry remain in effect even as we enter the 21st Century. The Queen of England remains the titular head of the Church of England, with vicarious powers to appoint bishops who then sit in the House of Lords. The separation of church (religion) and state, so much touted as an integral part of democracy, has been the exception rather than the rule throughout history. It remains elusive today even in such "democratic" nations as 21st century UK.

Is it a coincidence that Islam, perhaps the world's youngest major religion, embodies a greater degree of combining temporal and spiritual rulership, than do the other major religions? The Sultan or Emir or Sheik is not just a secular leader. He is also a spiritual leader. Friday prayers are not complete without homage and obeisance being paid to him. He administers sharia, a law of religious derivation. In this way, religion permeates everyday life and forms an intricate part of governance. Is this example from traditional Islam a better or worse formula for societal organization than the modern day western practice which assiduously tries to separate "church and state"? Is the separation of religious precepts from everyday life good or bad or neutral for society and its culture? What do we make of the fundamentalist Christians in the US who insist that religion should occupy a prominent place in the public/civic domain? Do these groups realize that what they are asking for is precisely what exists in sharia, a system which they scornfully disdain? These are all subjects of open debate.

There's one final corollary to the link between religion and ethnic units. Since a specific religion usually develops with and as part of the world view of an ethnic culture, it seems that most ethnic cultures evolve to be mono-religious in the first instance. The identity of the ethnic group is bound up with its religion. The situation probably remains so unless and until external forces introduce other religions into the culture.

17

Kaleidoscope Of *Truths*: Real, surreal, phony, or baloney

<u>***Context***</u>: *Written on 30 December 2005 in Punta Gorda, Belize.*

In the realm of the spiritual or metaphysical, the needle of what is true is hidden in a haystack of chaff. Every spiritual manifestation that we see or know has the possibility to be the real thing. It also has the possibility of being a spurious fake. Since we do not know and cannot know what the real thing is, we must allow for the possibility that one or more or none of the manifestations that we see is the real thing. We are free to perch on one of these possibilities (out of many), adopt it, believe it, and live by it. But however much we develop, embellish, sanctify, or elaborate our chosen possibility, it still remains only a possibility that could well be wrong. A traveler that is not pointed in the correct direction may go as fast as he wants. But the faster he goes, the farther he gets from the desired destination.

Given our human limitations, there is no way that we can transform our belief's possibility into a certainty. Take the question of life after death as an example. The only way you can know the truth for sure is by experience, i.e. by dying. Unfortunately, by the time you are qualified to know the truth, you are no longer able to communicate it to us the living. So, all evidence about what happens after death has to be circumstantial at best, and guesswork at worst. It's all hidden behind an impenetrable veil. Yet, the absence of concrete evidence has not stopped virtually every religious sect and ethnic group on earth from constructing its own scenario about what happens after we die. Most of these scenarios are passionately believed, and indeed form the bedrock of most major and minor religions. Needless to say, these sometimes conflicting scenarios cannot all be true. However, all the various religious manifestations on earth, from the dominant to the obscure, can each lay claim to being a possibility for the TRUTH. They cannot all be true since they conflict with one another, but each is a possibility.

A major line is crossed, though, when any of the religious persuasions lays claim to being a *certainty*. This is because the human condition does not permit us to know for sure what the certainty is, as illustrated by the example of what happens after death. The problem is that each religious faith on earth is like the bottom part of an hourglass. The contents filtering in from the heavenly upper portion have had to pass through the narrow straits of a human transmitter. The transmitter claims a divine revelation from the upper realm, and then transmits the revelation to the rest of us down here as an inspired writing or thought. Examples of such human transmitters abound: St. Paul for Christianity, Prophet Mohammed for Islam, Joseph Smith for Mormons, Moses for Judaism, Gautama for Buddhists, etc. Each of them claims that in a moment of supernatural enlightenment, they glimpsed the upper realm and were given messages to hand down to us. Even if we credit the original message with being pure and true, the fact that it has had to pass through fallible human hands and minds means that its purity could justifiably be in doubt. Where does divine perfection end and human fallibility begin? Lying between the upper and lower levels of the hourglass is the narrow strait of human intervention. Corruptibility and outright falsehood lurk in these straits. It requires a leap of faith to believe that what came from the upper realm (if indeed anything did) passed through the straits untainted and unadulterated.

A further tendency for tainting of the doctrinal truth arises from the fact that what society perceives as true keeps changing with time, and may conflict with previously-held "truths". As social and scientific changes transform societies from age to age, most religions are forced into an infinite series of rationalizations in order to cloak long-held "truths" in the garb of new-found realities. For example, eclipses, once seen as potent portents in religious circles, are now understood and explained away in scientific terms. But this means that happenings that were once attributed to spiritual ecliptic omens must now be explained in other ways. Similarly, some diseases that were once seen as divine visitations for sin might now be seen as microbial visitations for poor hygiene.

In many cases, the cloak that is fashioned and draped over old truths hardly fits. The cloak keeps getting adjusted and altered with time, until ultimately, the "truth" being cloaked bears little resemblance to what you started with. It is almost like a mathematical problem in which you are working from the answer, backwards. The first gauntlet thrown down by the sect, the first stake in the ground, is faith in a particular "truth". All subsequent observations that do not conform to this faith are discarded, modified, or suppressed in order to preserve the truthfulness of the "truth". The problem, of course, is that static doctrine of faith has difficulty continuing to ring true in the face of recently realized reality. Rather than discard the doctrine, most religions prefer to continue to fudge and obfuscate. For them, it is an existential course of action. It is the only way they can preserve the narrative that formed the raison d'être for their founding in the first place.

The truth is that I don't know the ultimate truth. Neither do you. Neither does anybody who is human. And you know that you don't know. So, why all the bravado in claiming and professing certainty? For those who profess certainty, the fallacious logic seems to be that the more ardently you believe in something, the more you increase its truthfulness. Or, that the greater the number of people that believe in something, the greater its veracity must be: everybody believes X; so X must be true. In contrast, common sense dictates that the degree of truth or falsehood of any assertion must lie in testing the assertion by itself, shorn of any emotion derived from the number and intensity of people that believe in it. Before the age of Copernicus and Galileo, virtually all people believed that the sun revolved around the earth. And this belief was held with such intensity that many people, including Galileo, who believed otherwise were persecuted for their contumacy. The intensity and pervasiveness of the mass belief did not alter the truth which only became evident later. However large you blow up a balloon to be, it is still all hot air. No matter how majestically high the hot-air balloon may soar, the reality check of a slight needle prick will cause its calamitous collapse and catastrophic crash.

Mass belief does little to move the goalposts of truth. Zero multiplied by one million still remains zero.

Still another line is crossed when any religious manifestation lays claim to being *exclusive*, i.e. the only possibility. Again, we are not capable of knowing this. One way of looking at things is to say that the ultimate truth (and possibly God) might be like a sea to which practically all rivers eventually flow. But the river courses vary. Confluences occur, and occasionally we have deltaic fragmentation. Each of the organized religions is but one of those rivers. We sail along our river with confidence, but not forgetting all those other rivers which could lead to the same sea.

Any religious persuasion that claims to be certain and exclusive (the only possibility) is making a double assertion that is beyond humans to know. Yet there is no shortage of religious sects that make this double claim. In the realm of the spiritual/metaphysical, everything is a possibility, but nothing is a certainty. And nothing, even if we concede certainty to it, can be exclusive in the sense of precluding other possibilities and certainties.

Incidentally, the claims of certainty and of being the only path to truth (exclusivity) are the ingredients that give rise to religious and political fundamentalism. This has happened through the ages, and continues to happen today. Indeed, certainty and exclusivity are mutually reinforcing. Once you are certain in your belief system, then all other belief systems are fake and only deserving of destruction or obliteration. But just as group A sees groups B and C as fake and destructible, so also does B see A and C as fake and undeserving of existence. And so on. It is not difficult to see how such religious fanaticism easily spirals into open conflict between groups of true believers, each group convinced (certain) of the rightness of their belief and cause.

If only each group were able to concede a slight margin of error in what they believe in. Such a margin not only tempers their own zealotry, but also allows them to see some possible positives in alternative views held by others. A little more humility on the part of the claimants would permit them to concede that some of the other paths just might have some element of truth as well.

18

Death, Orgasm, And God

__Context__: Written on 22 July, 1997 in Lae, Papua New Guinea.

What do death, orgasm, and God have in common? At first glance, nothing. However, it seems that death is to life, what orgasm is to sex, and perhaps what God is to humans. Each is a final end-point or limit. This prevents several situations from going on ad infinitum.

If the event of orgasm did not exist, then a sex act would go on and on and on, with nothing to define an end-point. The same can be said of life. If death did not exist to give it a definite endpoint, life would drag on and grind on indefinitely, with or without maintaining a tolerable quality. Similarly, for humans, the concept of God represents the embodiment of all things that are incomprehensible, unfathomable, and overwhelming; the end-point of all responsibility. The buck stops there.

19

Self-Determination Of Peoples: The case of *Anioma* identity, ethos, and strategic positioning

Context: *Many peoples around the world are going through the throes of self-determination. What sorts of issues do such peoples wrestle with? The case of the Anioma people of Nigeria illustrates the problems, prospects, and promises of the self-determination struggle. The Anioma, previously called "Western Ibo", are a people who speak Igbo-related dialects and live west of the River Niger in Nigeria's Delta State. The Enuani people are a central subset of the Anioma, and for purposes of this article, the two terms are used interchangeably. There has been long debate about Anioma origins and identity, especially how much or how little they share kinship with the main Igbo groups east of the Niger. A resolution of this debate has serious implications for the future political positioning of the Anioma people. The essay below is intended as a meaningful contribution to the ongoing debate. Although this discourse focuses on the Anioma people, much of it is applicable to all peoples everywhere who are grappling with issues of self-definition and self-determination. Written from 2011-2014.*

Introduction

To help you to understand the limits or extent of my expertise in addressing Anioma identity/ethos, some background about me seems pertinent. This will help you to appreciate where I am coming from, with my insights and possible blind spots. I am a true son of Anioma, born of an Oshimili father and an Aniocha mother. I spent the first six years of my life at Otolokpo in the Ika part of Anioma, and indeed started my schooling career there. The core of my childhood and the first decade of my life were spent entirely in village life in Anioma. After that, I lived deep in Igboland (Afikpo) for seven years of my adolescence. In my working life, I lived for 12 years as an adult at the cradle of Yorubaland (Ife), and lived for 13 years as a working professional in the Igbo heartland (Owerri). During all those years, I traveled and interacted extensively throughout Anioma, Igboland, and Yorubaland. From my upbringing, and in many decades as a professor of agricultural science, I have nurtured an abiding affinity for the down-to-earth aspects of our existence. Given this kind of background, much of what I have to say is derived from first-hand experience. I am not an ethnographer, anthropologist, or linguist; but I believe that my experience serves me well and gives me unique insights.

For starters, let me share some of the insights that my experience has given me concerning the major ethnic groups in Nigeria, especially the Yoruba and Igbo. To the outsider, the Yoruba appear to be a homogeneous monolithic group. However, when you live among them, you appreciate that the Yoruba are indeed a conglomerate of Egba, Ijesha, Eko (Lagos), Ijebu, Oyo, Ekiti, Akoko, Okun, etc. While many trace their mythical origin to Ife, there are significant groups that have come from other places, joined the conglomerate, and shed their previous affiliation and language. The indigenous Eko (Lagos) people, for example, trace their origins to migration from Benin; but today they are considered part and parcel of Yorubaland. As far as I know, no Eko person denies that they are Yoruba just because of their non-Yoruba origin.

The various components of the Yoruba conglomerate share certain cultural traits, the most obvious of which is mutual intelligibility of their dialects, especially if spoken slowly. There are commonalities in the dialects, but there are significant differences as well, so much so that an

Akoko person can only just barely make sense of the Egba dialect; and so on. Fortunately for the Yoruba, early contact with western civilization and other factors enabled them decades ago to develop and promote a standardized central dialect (Oyo) which serves as a meeting point or lingua franca for the other dialects.

Just like the Yoruba, what the outsider sees as a monolithic Igboland is indeed a conglomerate of the peoples of Ngwa, Nsukka, Abiriba, Ukwa, Ezza, Ehugbo (Afikpo), Owerri, Awka, Orlu, Aguleri, Ogbaru, etc.etc. Again, the spoken dialect of each of these groups is distinct and different from that of the others. The villager from Awka would need to strain to comprehend the village dialect of Abiriba, or Nsukka, or Ukwa. Yet, there are enough linguistic and cultural commonalities for them all to be lumped together as Igbo. Unlike the Yoruba, the Igbo made a late start in promoting a common dialect (Ohunhun/Umuahia/Owerri) for all to embrace.

Again, like the Yoruba, what we know as Igboland has been the beneficiary of migrations from other ethnic groups, mainly Edo from the west, Igala and Idoma from the north, Ibibio/Efik from the east, and Ijaw from the south. Again, each migrating group has integrated and folded itself into its new abode, and is now no less Igbo than the other groups.

So, we can either say that there is no such thing as Yoruba or Igbo because of the many different groups that in-migrated to make up the entity, or we accept that each entity is a heterogeneous conglomerate that has been significantly infused with in-migrants from different places at different times.

Now let's look at Anioma. It is incontestable that the people that make up Anioma have come from different non-Anioma places. Anioma lore and myth are full of examples. Modern scholars have given credence to many of such claims (e.g. Mordi, E. N. and Opone, P. O. (2009) Origins and Migrations of the Enuani People of South Central Nigeria Reconsidered. *Stud Tribes Tribals* 7[1]: 47-56.). But does the fact that much of Illah came from Igala make it any less part of Anioma today? Does the fact that Agbor came from Benin make it any less part of Anioma? So it is with the Ezechima clan (Obomkpa, Onicha-Olona, Obior, etc); so with Obiarukwu; so with Aboh. The point is that two things happened after the in-migrants arrived: (1) they shed parts of their previous culture, most significantly their language; and (2) they adopted the norms and language of those around them, mostly earlier-arriving people from Nri/Igboland. So, having originated in Anioma is not a pre-requisite for being part of Anioma today, nor is it required that they should have originated from a particular outside (non-Anioma) place. Even if every town/village in Anioma originated outside Anioma (i.e. if none originated within Anioma), all of them would still be considered genuine parts of Anioma today. Similarly, having originated in Igboland should not be a pre-requisite for being part of today's Igbo conglomerate. Even if every Anioma community originated outside of Igboland (i.e. if none originated in Igboland), that does not speak to whether or not they could be considered part of Igboland today. Incidentally, some of the larger communities in Anioma indisputably trace their origins to Igboland, for example Ogwashi, Igbuzo, Owa Clan, etc. Should we cut these out of Anioma because they are undeniably of Igbo origin?

Anioma Origins and Strategy: Multi-point commentary

S everal writers go to great lengths to show that only a small part of Anioma originated in Igboland. They might well be correct in this assertion. However, they go on to conclude that because most Anioma people migrated from places besides Igboland, Anioma cannot be considered as part of today's Igbo conglomerate. The logic for this conclusion is flawed. Here are some of the reasons why, as well as other insights into the Anioma condition:

1. As argued above, the source of the in-migration is never the determinant of whether a group is today considered Igbo or Yoruba. Otherwise, large slices of both groups would be disqualified, including large segments of the Eko, Afikpo, Nsukka, Abiriba, Onitsha, Oguta, Ogbaru, etc. Similarly, and rightly so, the source of in-migration is not a determinant for being part of Anioma today. Otherwise, you disqualify Agbor, Ebu, Ogwashi, the entire Ezechima clan, Igbuzo, Illah, Owa etc. etc. Why then should the source of in-migration be a determinant for being part of today's Igbo conglomerate? Indeed, for most Igbo groups, we do not use it as a determinant. If Ogbaru, Abiriba, Afikpo, Oguta, Onitsha,

etc. cannot disclaim membership of the Igbo conglomerate just because they originally migrated from elsewhere outside Igboland, why should Anioma be entitled to such a disclaimer? We cannot have it both ways.

2. Let's look at Anioma itself. How homogeneous is it? Certainly, it breaks down into three major linguistic groups: Aniocha/Oshimili, Ika, and Ukwuani/Aboh. Spoken at normal speed, these dialects are just barely mutually comprehensible. As one who speaks Aniocha/Oshimili, I recall with embarrassment how I struggled to make conversation at village markets in Abbi and Emu-Unor in the Ukwuani area. Indeed, the uneducated villager in Obior, raised in the Aniocha dialect, is probably more comfortable with the Ogidi dialect across the Niger than with the Ukwuani dialect. Yet, Ogidi is uncontestably in Igboland (outside Anioma), while Ukwuani is in Anioma with Obior. Is it therefore honest to claim a greater affinity between the Anioma dialects than between Aniocha and Ogidi? The truth is that even Anioma itself is a conglomerate. Each of its dialects is distinct in itself. Given that the Anioma dialects differ from one another, the fact that they also differ from those across the Niger does not disqualify them from belonging to the same larger group as the cross-Niger dialects. As already pointed out, the linguistic differences between segments of acknowledged Igboland (e.g. between Awka and Ukwa) can be greater than those between parts of Anioma and Igboland. In short, we can infer that each Anioma dialect is distinct *within* Anioma but not apart from Anioma; similarly, the Anioma dialects can be considered as distinct within the Igbo conglomerate, but not apart from it.

3. The heterogeneity of Anioma is also reflected in the varying intensity of fervor with which the various Anioma components embrace the very concept of Anioma identity, and the pursuit of an Anioma State. Enthusiasm for the Anioma identity is strongest in Aniocha/Oshimili, but fades precipitously as you move to Ika, and then fades some more in Ukwuani/Aboh. I have yet to attend an Anioma gathering, both at home and in the diaspora, that is not numerically overwhelmed by Aniocha/Oshimili persons. Again, a history of political separation is a factor here. While Aniocha/

Oshimili and Ika were together in the colonial Asaba Division within Benin Province, Ukwuani/Aboh were not even in the same Province, talk less the same Division. But perhaps a more potent factor in the disparity of support for Anioma identity today is the fear of domination. This time, it is an intra-Anioma fear by the others that they will be dominated by the Aniocha/Oshimili axis.

4.   Professional linguists and ethnographers classify the Anioma dialects as part of the greater Igbo group of dialects. The question is often asked: if the Anioma people migrated from various non-Igbo places, how come the language is closest to Igbo, and is no longer intelligible to the places they migrated from? A migrating people do not suddenly drop their language and adopt another one unless there's a serious circumstance. The most logical answer is that these people migrated into an area that already had other people with a lingua franca (Igbo), and that with time, the migrants became assimilated. The academic paper by Mordi and Opone (2009) lends credence to this theory. There is also historical evidence that much of the area occupied by today's Anioma was part of the Nri/Igbo hegemony for centuries before migrants started arriving from Benin and elsewhere. This explains why the migrants adopted a language and culture similar to Igbo, while retaining vestiges of their previous culture. If they did not migrate into an Igbo-speaking area, there is no way they would have dropped their previous language and adopted an Igbo-related language. And of course, there was extensive genetic mixing between the migrants and the endemic Igbo population, so that today's Anioma people are not pure descendants of the places they migrated from. They have both genetic and cultural affinity to the Igbo.

5.   The Olukumi and Igala-speaking towns in Anioma, so elaborately cited by many writers, would appear to be an exception. But they really are not. I have visited every Olukumi town (Ugbodu, Ukwu-Nzu, Ubulubu, Idumu-Ogo, Inyogo), each of them many times. I have also spent long periods in the Igala-speaking town of Ebu. For several years in my childhood, I happened to live at Idumuje-Uno, one mile from Ugbodu (an Olukumi town). I went to Ugbodu to sell produce nearly every market day, and

we occasionally went to Ugbodu's Ohe stream to fetch water. I interacted extensively with Olukumi people on their own turf. The fact is that in addition to being atypical and few, these Olukumi communities are geographically at the extreme northern fringe of Anioma, wedged in the case of Ugbodu between Ishan and the rest of Anioma. Indeed, when you go down to Ugbodu's Ohe stream, you walk across and suddenly you've left Anioma in Delta State. You're now in Ishan-land in Edo State. Anyway, this isolated existence would have enabled the Olukumi and similar groups to resist assimilation longer than peoples that migrated into the heart of Anioma. What we are seeing in these places is an intermediate stage of the assimilation process, frozen in time. Most Olukumi people today are bilingual, speaking an Anioma dialect in addition to their Yoruba-like dialect which they brought along when they in-migrated. Furthermore, many family and person names in these towns are similar, not to Yoruba, but to the names in neighboring Anioma towns. Names like Okwechime, Okonkwo, etc. are the norm in Ugbodu, Ukwu-Nzu and Ubulubu. Similarly, Ikenye, Okolie, etc. are common in Igala-speaking Ebu which is equally at the northern fringe of Anioma. Assimilation has taken hold in these communities, and if there is not a deliberate effort to blunt it, Olukumi people of the next century might be linguistically indistinguishable from their surrounding Anioma neighbors.

6. One of the arguments used to support the non-Igbo connection for Anioma is the fact that Anioma people have suffered much at the hands of the Igbo people across the Niger. Some cite the atrocities that occurred during the Nigerian civil war, and the fact that the easterners have been lukewarm in their support for the creation of Anioma State. But the point remains that the suspicion with which Anioma people view the easterners is fully reciprocated among the easterners who worry about the lukewarm affiliation that Anioma people show towards the greater Igbo conglomerate. The attitude is mutually ambivalent, mutually suspicious, and mutually opportunistic. It is also mutually harmful. What we have is a vicious circle that works against Anioma strategic interests, and will continue to hurt the Anioma people if it is not addressed.

7. If the attitude to, and treatment of, the Anioma people is a qualifier for identity with them, then some of the other places which are being credited as the sources of the Anioma people are even less qualified than Igboland. Let's take Edoland (Bini), the favorite source adduced for origins of Anioma people. How did the Anioma people fare among the Bini's during the civil war? Were they not the victims of a pogrom there? And what about the Owegbe (Bini) cults that were used to neutralize the pioneer Mid-West government of Osadebay, a son of Anioma? Going beyond Edoland, what about Yorubaland, the much glamorized source of the Olukumi as detailed above? How did the Anioma people fare in the Yoruba-dominated Western Region? And again, how did the Yoruba treat Anioma persons and interests during the civil war? The examples go on, up to the present-day political emasculation of the Anioma people through domination by the Urhobo. Let us not forget the historical fact that many of the people migrating to Anioma from these places had fallen foul of the authorities in the places they emigrated from; or they feared for their security. Far from being a matter of comfortable choice, migration was often undertaken under duress or even outright expulsion. In such cases, the migrants sought to distance themselves from their origins in many ways: physically, culturally, and emotionally. The point here is not to fan the flames of animosity or dislike for these other peoples surrounding Anioma. They are our neighbors for ever, and we must develop *modus vivendi* accommodations that enable us to live with them in peace. Instead, the main point here is that all the touted sources of Anioma migration have moved on. They have moved on to a point where the Anioma people are definitely outsiders to whom no favors are owed.

8. When all these groups and other outsiders look at Anioma people, what do they see? It is not for nothing that the rest of the country and the rest of the world see the Anioma people as a subset of the larger Igbo conglomerate. I've never heard the Anioma people being referred to as Eastern-Edo or Northern-Urhobo, or Eastern-Yoruba, or Southern-Ishan. All the appellations that the rest of the world uses for the Anioma people are qualified versions of "Igbo":

Western-Igbo; Bendel-Igbo; Ika-Igbo, etc. Why so? Whether or not we like it or admit it, this is because they see the cultural and linguistic affinity which exists between Anioma and Igboland, but which does not exist to the same extent between Anioma and the other touted sources of Anioma origins. No untutored Anioma person can understand Edo, Ishan, Yoruba or Urhobo; but they can understand Onitsha, Ogidi, Oguta, Nnewi, Orlu, etc., albeit with difficulty. Irrespective of their origins, today's Anioma people are seen as having adopted a language and culture that is more identifiable with Igbo than with any other ethnic group on earth. So, like it or not, want it or not, the rest of the country and the world are telling the Anioma that they are Igbo, albeit a qualified kind of Igbo. Not surprisingly, the socio-political destiny of the Anioma people has been inexorably linked with that of the Igbo. In the frequent anti-Igbo pogroms that have occurred in northern Nigeria before and since the civil war, the perpetrators made no distinction between Anioma and non-Anioma Igbo people. They saw no distinction, and any confronted Anioma person who tried to make that distinction probably met the same unpleasant fate as all other Igbos. The perpetrators of the pogroms saw any attempts at fine distinctions simply as hair-splitting that only deserved their spitting. To them, and to most of the outside world, the Anioma are part of the Igbo conglomerate. Period. End of story. Some might even say, get over it and move on. This is a fact of life which many Anioma people are yet to reconcile themselves with.

9. Some Anioma indigenes even want to jettison the name Anioma because it sounds like Igbo. What then do they propose to do with the person names of Anioma people, virtually all of which sound like Igbo? Just like the camel with its head in the tent and the main body outside, do we throw away the Anioma label because it sounds Igbo and yet continue to carry around our Igbo-sounding person names? And what of the Anioma dialects themselves, all of which have a likeness to Igbo and to no other language on earth? Changing all that, just to run away from being identified with the Igbo, would entail revisionism on a mammoth scale that would eviscerate the current language and culture of the Anioma people.

The irony of the situation is this: denying that Anioma is part of the Igbo conglomerate has not endeared Anioma to the rest of the country which believes otherwise. Yet, such denial has seriously antagonized the cross-Niger Igbo people.

10. This denial has increased exponentially since the Igbo lost the civil war. During the first republic when the denial was less in evidence, Anioma was the beneficiary of the political clout of the Igbo at the national level. Osadebay and the champions of the Mid-West region unabashedly aligned themselves with, and benefitted from, the national heft of Zik and other Igbo politicians. This alliance delivered a measure of success that resulted in the creation of the Mid-West region. With the post-war tide of Igbo-denial now sweeping through Anioma, the collective Igbo weight in national politics has been antagonized. The Igbo caucus has therefore been reluctant to lend its full support to the Anioma State effort, or even to champion developmental causes of the Anioma people (like the siting of universities and facilities). It is a forlorn hope for the Anioma people to expect any other ethnic group to substitute for the Igbo as the champions of the Anioma people at the national level. Having defined the Anioma people as part of the Igbo conglomerate, the rest of the country expects Anioma to live by that definition and sink or swim accordingly. All this calls for a critical re-examination of the strategic alliances that Anioma people need in order to facilitate their interests at the national stage. However much they are despised at the national level, the Igbo remain the only significant ethnic collective that can champion Anioma interests nationally. Anioma needs to strategically reposition itself to make this happen. The current formula is not working.

11. Since the civil war which put serious brakes on Igbo ascendancy, the Igbo-denying culture has become fashionable even among groups that previously touted their Igbo-ness. It is a revisionist streak that is definitely present in Anioma. For Anioma, it is driven by at least four factors: (a) a history of political separation from the main Igbo groups; (b) physical separation by the Niger River; (c) fear of domination by the eastern Igbo; and (d) reluctance to

identify with the loser in the civil war. The same civil war spawned a similar Igbo-denying ethos among the Ikwere around Igwe-Ocha [Port Harcourt], Rivers State. It is not surprising that the rapid decline of the Igbo socio-political fortunes in recent decades has coincided with a similar decline in Anioma, and has been a major factor fueling the Igbo-distancing tendency in Anioma. One may say that the Anioma decline has been exacerbated because Anioma is viewed with distrust by the rest of Igboland, and with Igbo-targeting disdain by the rest of the country. This is a serious case of double jeopardy with very real consequences. Such is the dilemma in which Anioma finds itself; a veritable vicious circle. It reminds me of the dilemma of a light-skinned Negro family in the old segregated south in the USA. The family claimed that they were not black, and therefore did not bother to develop social bonds with the black community. But the larger [white-majority] community saw them as black and treated them as such. When the white segregationists started their rampage, where did this black-denying family seek refuge? They were humiliatingly forced to flee for cover among the same black organizations that they had disdained and distanced. The right of self-definition is there, but the definition of the wider community is a fact of life that cannot be ignored. Similarly, Richard Nixon got up and famously declared, "I'm not a crook!" This did not necessarily absolve him from being a crook in everybody else's eyes. Such are the limits of self-definition. No matter how much Anioma people shout that they are not part of the Igbo conglomerate, the rest of the nation and the rest of the world have always begged to differ.

12. Within Anioma, the term "Igbo" is often used colloquially to refer to the Igbo people across the Niger, as separate from Anioma people. To the Anioma, it is a pejorative term that conveys elements of industriousness, exploitativeness, cunning, and parsimony as perceived in some cross-Niger Igbo. It is noteworthy, however, that some groups that the Anioma would refer to as (cross-Niger) Igbo also have a colloquial use of "Igbo" that excludes themselves. This is most noticeable among the Onitsha, but also exists among the Ogbaru, Oguta, Ukwa, Ikwere, etc. The point here is that

the colloquial use of "Igbo" does not constitute an authoritative definition of who is Igbo [Question: Was or was not Nnamdi Azikiwe of Onitsha considered the leader of the Igbo people in his prime? Yet Onitsha has a colloquial use of "Igbo" that excludes Onitsha people]. In reality, once the matter is looked at in the larger Nigerian or global context, even these groups that see the Igbo as "the other" begin to concede their common cultural and linguistic bond to the Igbo conglomerate. They see an Igbo universe which includes them. Even at the grassroots level, for example, the "Igbo Unions" in Yorubaland or Hausaland have historically included active members from areas that colloquially see "Igbo" as the other. Even as I write this (2011), an Anioma son, Chief Uwechue of Ogwashi-Uku, is the president of the global apex Igbo cultural body, the *Ohanaeze Ndigbo*. The situation is almost analogous the use of the term "Yankee". There is a sense in which it includes all U.S. Americans (as in "Yankee go home"), and a narrower sense in which persons in the U.S. South would insist that they are not Yankees. So, to many Anioma people, there is ambivalence in the use of the word "Igbo": there is one sense of the word which excludes themselves, and another sense which includes them.

13. The establishment of a strong Anioma identity is extremely important. No question about that, and no compromises on that. But there is no inconsistency about a strongly-identified Anioma being part of a larger entity. There is no zero-sum game here. Some have argued that being seen as part of a larger conglomerate (Igbo) would militate against Anioma identity and self-determination. Not so. There are many valid counter-arguments to this. First, Anioma is currently defined as part of Delta State, but that does not in any way diminish Anioma integrity or cause it to lose its identity. It is seen as a part of Delta State which in turn is seen as a part of Nigeria. Similarly, Owa is seen as part of Ika, which in turn is seen as part of Anioma. We encourage Ika to identify with Anioma, while at the same time developing a strong sense of identity for Ika. We do not see a strong Ika identity as conflicting with Ika's identification with Anioma, or with the effort to carve out an Anioma identity. The point here is that each of us belongs to

a series of progressively enlarging concentric units, each of which can self-determine a strong identity, without detracting from the other. Hence, Ika people are defined as a unique ethno-cultural entity that is part of Anioma, but that definition does not interfere with their own identity or self-determination. Delta State being defined as part of Nigeria, or Nigeria as part of Africa, in no way erodes the integrity or identity of the unit being defined. Why then would we suppose that Anioma's identity and self-determination would be lost if the facts on the ground cause it to be defined as part of the Igbo conglomerate? In any case, what is the singular trait that the Anioma people have in common that separates them from all the other peoples of Delta State? Is it not their Igbo-related dialect/culture? How could we then turn around to have an identity that denies that connection?

14. Secondly, the definition of Anioma identity is based on facts, not wishes. And the definition is not being foisted on Anioma or championed by the sinister agenda of external entities. It is based the incontrovertible facts on the ground, mainly what Anioma itself presents to the world as its culture, language, and customs. It is based on the snapshot of the situation as it exists today. The definition is an objective exercise, and must be distinctly separated from what we wish to do going forward. A man that was born by my mother is my brother, based on the facts of the situation. The definition is based on objective fact, and does not change, whether I like him or not. However, I still reserve the right going forward to relate to him or to stay distant from him. In either case, he still remains my brother by definition. To claim otherwise would be a disservice to the facts and to history. So, accepting that Anioma is part of an Igbo conglomerate is only an acceptance of the facts on the ground; it does not necessarily pre-determine how closely or how distantly Anioma should relate to other Igbo sub-groups or to the larger conglomerate. Who we are has been determined for us by the *objective* facts on the ground; who we want to be is the *subjective* focus of our current debate.

15. Anioma's hybrid position has been a huge source of ambivalence. Like the mythical bat, we are neither birds of the air nor mammals

of the ground. As happened during the civil war, this situation has enabled Anioma people to bestraddle both sides: suffering at the hands of both sides, and benefitting at the hands of both sides. A similar fate has characterized Anioma for much of Nigeria's political existence. This situation challenges Anioma to think critically and strategically. How do we maximize the benefits from both sides, while minimizing the adverse blowback from both sides? For example, how do we tap into the industriousness/resilience of the Igbo, and their national political clout, without evoking negative sentiments or inheriting some of their negative baggage? Going forward, Anioma still reserves the right to carve its own identity and self-determination as distinct from other members of the conglomerate. But in doing so, Anioma has to be strategically careful to build pragmatic coalitions, while avoiding the creation of enemies.

16. As Anioma struggles with its contradictions and wrestles with its identity, its political, cultural, and economic bases are badly in need of buttressing. And the buttressing cannot wait until the identity debate plays out. The debate over identity should not delay the development of concrete strategies to tackle the problems of Anioma. Whichever way Anioma eventually defines itself, it needs now, and will continue to need, alliances and coalitions with other groups and sub-groups in order to leverage its efforts. It would be a strategic mistake if Anioma, in the process of defining itself, should alienate or antagonize other groups that could potentially serve as allies in the long-term Anioma interests. We should always be about building bridges. You can never have too many friends.

Anioma Ethos

While the debate rages about Anioma origins, it is pertinent to observe certain characteristics that mark the Anioma ethos. These characteristics can best be summarized with the acronym SUPA: Satisfied, Unambitious, Poor, and Arrogant.

"*Satisfied*" means that the Anioma person generally has an outlook of contentment in life. This means that he is prone to being happy even in the face of difficult life circumstances.

Perhaps resulting from being easily contented, the Anioma person is generally *unambitious,* bordering on indolence. Where his kin from east of the Niger is hustling and scraping to get ahead, the Anioma person is more likely to stand back and contentedly wonder what the fuss is all about. The unindustrious, almost lazy, attitude of the Anioma person contrasts with the trade-mark industriousness and craftiness of the eastern Igbo.

Given the lack of hustle, it is not surprising that the typical Anioma person is *poor.* Despite the huge amount of natural resources with which they are endowed, the Anioma people generally live in penury. Worse still, the political cohesiveness that is needed to lift them out of poverty has been constantly frustrated by a sense of contentment and a false feeling of security. This has enabled the poverty to persist and propagate from generation to generation.

If you expect a people that are poor and unindustrious to be humble, the Anioma people surprise you with the opposite. Both individually and collectively, the Anioma people are a very proud people, some might say *arrogant.* Other adjectives that have been used include haughty, conceited, and unbowed. Poor-and-proud is one way to describe the Anioma people. Many jobs that other people accept and do, the Anioma youth would disdain and consider to be infra dig, beneath their dignity. The goodly gofer life is certainly not for them. As a result, most of the artisan jobs in the Anioma area are performed, not by Anioma persons, but by artisans from other ethnic groups, mostly the eastern Igbo and the Urhobo. Meanwhile, hordes of Anioma youth are roaming the streets, looking pretty, and sneering superciliously at those doing the artisan jobs. This ethos of no-hustle arrogance is shared by the Onitsha, Ogbaru, and Oguta people, three Anioma-related groups that happen to live east of the Niger.

One final trait which Anioma people have manifested in recent decades needs to be mentioned. It is the ease with which they are willing to cast away key elements of their culture. We can illustrate this with *akwa ocha,* the native white cloth which is worn toga-like by the men and as a waist wrapper by the women. For centuries, this cloth has been the identifying garb of most Anioma people (with the possible exception of some in the Ndokwa/Aboh axis). It has been their sartorial totem through the ages, woven by Anioma people and worn by them with pomp and pride. No other attire occupies this position. Yet, it is alarming the extent to which

Anioma people have abandoned *akwa ocha* in the last half century and replaced it with clothing borrowed from other lands.

The first stage in the abandonment occurred in the second half of the 20th century when fewer and fewer Anioma people undertook the weaving of the cloth. The art of weaving *akwa ocha* progressively became a lost art among the Anioma people. The vacuum created was filled by the non-Anioma Igbira people from around Okene in Kogi State, a long distance away from the heart of Anioma. The Igbira produced delicately decorated *akwa ocha* specifically targeted for the Anioma markets. By the end of the 20th century, virtually all the *akwa ocha* sold in local markets in Anioma were produced in Igbiraland. Anioma people did not take notice of this anomalous shift in the base of production, or probably did not care.

The second stage in the abandonment of *akwa ocha* is currently in progress (2014). Having already lost interest in producing *akwa ocha*, the Anioma now seem to be losing interest in wearing it, even on culturally-significant occasions. How many times have we been to gatherings of Anioma people where hardly anybody is wearing *akwa ocha*. Most are decked out in Yoruba-style agbada and cap. They do look nice in the agbada attire, but they would also have looked nice in three-piece Savile Row suits from London. The point here has nothing to do with looks; it has everything to do with the abandonment of your identity in favor of somebody else's. To make matters worse, even Anioma traditional rulers, the ultimate guardians of Anioma culture, are equally guilty of this abandonment. How many times do we see official gatherings of Anioma traditional rulers where most are clad in agbada or similar garbs that are borrowed from outside Anioma? Are they not aware that Anioma people look up to them to uphold Anioma culture, including their dressing culture? If the culture guardians are complicit in the abandonment of *akwa ocha*, what do they expect of the general populace? As Chaucer asked: If gold rust, what then will iron do?

The abandonment of *akwa ocha* is probably symptomatic of the general decay and neglect infesting Anioma culture. Hopefully, this treatise will serve as a clarion wake-up call alerting Anioma people to the endangered status of their supposedly beloved *akwa ocha*. Hopefully, there will be a rallying to uphold this unique aspect of Anioma culture. According to the Anioma saying, if you decline to lick your lips to protect them from the dry harmattan wind, who do you expect to lick your lips for you? If Anioma people fail to patronize the *akwa ocha* that has been their age-old cultural identity, who do they expect to uphold this unique aspect of their culture for them?

In conclusion, I welcome the spirit of debate about Anioma origins, identity, and culture. The above discourse should be considered an integral part of the debate. Hopefully, the debate will move on from issues of identity to issues of strategy, and how Anioma can build coalitions for its own betterment. This debate should also serve as tonic inspiration for other peoples around the globe who are struggling with their own issues of self-determination.

20

The Innocent Civilian And Democratic Responsibility

__Context__: Written on 31 December (New Year's Eve), 2002, in Chambersburg, PA, USA.

When there is conflict between nations, civilians are usually caught up in the ensuing strife. We usually refer to such people as innocent civilians. But how innocent is the "innocent civilian" that we hear so much about?

Let us take two contrasting nations, A and B. Nation A is democratic, and the rulers are answerable to the people. The people in turn can influence the policies and actions of their rulers through regular elections and robust feedback mechanisms. In addition, the citizens of A can control the activities of their corporations through their ownership of stocks and shares. Corporate boards implement policies that the shareholders want and can support with their share votes. The boards risk being replaced if they should propagate policies that the shareholders do not support. Nation B, on the other hand, is autocratic. The people have little or no say in governance or in the policies of the rulers. And the commanding heights of business are monopolized by an oligarchic elite, answerable to nobody else but themselves. Nation A fits the model of what most developed western societies claim to be. To them, their claim to being democratic is hinged on the ability of the people to exercise control over the government and over the business sector. In contrast, Nation B is undemocratic because the people have little power or control over the government or the business sector. Nation B more closely resembles the typical struggling less-developed country.

If government policies in Nation A are causing conflict with B, each citizen of A is fractionally responsible for that policy, since they have the power to influence or change it. They cannot brandish their democratic credential, with its empowerment of ordinary people, and at the same time claim powerlessness in the face of odious government policies. You cannot eat your cake and have it. Your democratic claim to control the government saddles you with vicarious responsibility for the good and bad actions of the government. In contrast, the citizens of Nation B have a legitimate claim to powerlessness. Since they do not have much say in their own governance, they can legitimately claim exoneration from the misdeeds of their government. They bear little or no responsibility, since they are powerless to influence their government or its policies.

In a situation where the citizens of A support and encourage their government along the path of bad policies towards B, their culpability is even greater. The people of B are likely to lament the bad policies of the government in A. But they take it one step further. The people of B will see each citizen of A as bearing a significant responsibility for the bad policy of their government which they have installed and can influence. If the bad policy of A happens to be to the detriment of B, then the citizens of B may feel tempted to retaliate against the individual citizens of A, whom they hold indirectly culpable. Unfair as it may seem, this is what often leads to the "innocent" citizens of A being the targets of actions and aggression from the citizens of B. The people of B see the citizens of A not as "innocent" civilians, but as props which enable their government to perpetrate and perpetuate policies that are harmful. The same goes for the malfeasance of multinational companies that have their origins in Nation A.

Even when open hostility breaks out between A and B, the ordinary citizens of both countries are adversely impacted as collateral damage. They may suffer killing, maiming, displacement, hunger, and other incidental afflictions of war. Those who suffer in this way in country B are much closer to the definition of "innocent" victims, given their powerlessness to influence their government's policy in the first place. But the adversely impacted persons in A have less of a claim to innocence, given their vicarious role in supporting and encouraging bad policies in their elected leaders. They have a power to change bad policies, and are complicit if they do not exercise that power. The average person in B does not have such power and suffers doubly: at the hands of their own oppressive government, and at the hands of the government of A. While all collateral damage is detestable, that inflicted on the B person is morally much more reprehensible. Conversely, the persons in country A must constantly exercise their power to control their government and institutions, including multinational corporations. That is an inescapable responsibility of living in a democratic country. Should they be passive in the exercise of that responsibility, they must know that they cannot evade the culpability that flows from such passivity.

21

Hypocrisy Is Asymmetrical
And Two-Faced

Context: *Written on various dates from 1997 to 2002.*

Hypocrisy is one of the most galling manifestations in human interactions. History is full of grandiose people who place themselves on high pedestals, superciliously disdaining other people, while secretly wallowing in muck. Remember how the ancient Romans saw themselves as sitting at the height of human civilization? And how they considered most other known societies as barbarians? Yet, they presided over an empire where they entertained themselves by watching wild beasts tear up human beings. To us today, that would be the height of barbarity. But it was not barbarous to them because the powers of the empire defined it as acceptable. For the same reason, their highly stratified slave-ridden society was not barbarous; nor was the torturing and crucifixion of criminals. Not only were people outside the empire considered barbarians, but even within the empire, non-citizens were subject to inferior treatment. As happened in the case of St. Paul, citizens were entitled to a fair trial, but non-citizens within the same nation were denied due process, up to and including death by stoning without trial. Similar glaring cases of hypocrisy by self-glorifying empires are not unknown in our world today.

For people who do not claim a moral high ground, it is fairly easy to tolerate hypocrisy. But when an individual, organization, or country claims a moral high ground, then they invite a more critical analysis of their credentials as it relates to hypocrisy. There is nothing more repugnant than when the sanctimoniously rich and powerful display manifest hypocrisy in their dealings with others. They seem to be saying, "I will do as I like, but will use force if necessary to prevent you from doing as I do." The western powers in today's world are unfortunately guilty of such a stance. Every part of the world is probably guilty as well, but the guilt of the West is all the more glaring because of their claim to a moral high ground from which they preach to the rest. It is a case of pernicious exceptionalism.

Americans (and some other western countries) often wonder why their nation cannot find love among so many peoples around the world. *Why do they hate us*, they ask? The truth is that some of the hatred has its roots in the hypocrisy that many of these other peoples perceive in global American behavior. Hypocrisy does not engender love. It has the opposite effect. Recognizing and addressing cases of hypocrisy will go a long way in improving the image and affection that peoples around the world have for America. Pointing out and discussing such hypocrisy should be seen as a positive contribution.

A few examples of western hypocrisy are discussed below.

1. *Britain in Hong Kong [Written 17 July 1997 as Britain was gearing up to hand back Hong Kong to China]*

The British ruled Hong Kong for over 150 years. For virtually all of that time, there was no democracy. Only colonialism, dictated from London. The consent of the governed was irrelevant. All important laws and policies were imported from London. Then suddenly, on eve of the handover to China, the British introduced "democratic" reforms which they are insisting that China must adopt and maintain. What hypocrisy!

At any rate, how did the British get Hong Kong in the first place? It was through the Opium Wars in which the British manifested one of history's most disgraceful cases of state-sponsored drug-pushing. The British even backed up the practice with military insistence that another people (the Chinese) must consume drugs even though those people did not want to. What a shame, especially in the face of the holier-than-thou attitude of today's western powers to the drug problem. Today, they prefer to cast blame for the problem elsewhere: they prefer to blame and punish third world countries who produce the drugs, rather than blame/punish their own selves who create the demand and consume the drugs. I wonder what would happen if third world consumers of cigarettes threaten sanctions on developed countries if they did not stop the production and exportation of cigarettes. Similarly, what would happen if Islamic countries threatened harm to western countries if they did not stop the production and exportation of alcohol? We in the West expect to produce all the alcohol we want, and let each country around the world determine how much of it their populace consumes. By the same logic, the onus for reducing drug consumption should fall on the consuming countries in the first instance. The consuming countries should be doing more at home to reduce the demand, rather than the hypocritical scapegoating of the producing countries.

Even Australia, of all countries, joined in the western refrain condemning China for its human rights record, and threatening retribution. Given the history of Australia's treatment of the aborigines, how can the pot be calling the kettle black? And how could they so easily forget the "Australia for the whites" policy which excluded non-white immigration to Australia up till the 1970's? I guess if you are "western", you have a birthright to enthrone yourself on the pedestal from which you can bully others. It is this same Australia that recently (1990's) refused to sign a trade pact with the European Union because the EU insisted on a human rights clause.

Anyway, as Mr. Patten (Hong Kong's last British Governor) kept carrying on about "democracy" and his attempt to preserve it in the face of Chinese attempts to destroy it, I kept asking myself, "Who elected Mr. Patten?" Of course nobody did, least of all the people of Hong Kong. His presence there was the ultimate travesty of democracy. Indeed, you may ask, "Who elected Mr. Patten's head of state, the Queen?" That's democracy for you!

2. *Labor mobility [18 July 1997]:*

Three key elements for economic productivity are goods, capital, and labor. Developed countries insist that they want open markets and competition. These are touted as the pillars of capitalism. Great! In the spirit of promoting competition, they insist on flooding the developing countries with what they have to offer – mainly manufactured goods which can out-compete those made locally in the poor countries. When it comes to manufactured goods, the rich countries certainly have a lot to offer. They also have a near-monopoly on capital, the second key element for economic productivity. With the World Bank and the International Monetary Fund carefully engineered to do their bidding, the developed countries have comfortably cornered the market on global capital.

But what do the less-developed countries have to offer? Their forte, it seems, is labor, the third key element for economic productivity. They have labor and not just that; they offer labor that is abundant and competitively priced. So, does the much-touted spirit of open markets and competition extend to the acceptance of the cheaper labor which the developing countries have to offer? Mostly not! The cheap labor, skilled or unskilled, must stay quarantined within each poor country, and must not be allowed to infest the richer countries.

It seems that the dogma of open markets/competition is thrust forward only when it suits the developed countries. Their manufactured goods and capital are free to go anywhere and compete, but such freedom is denied to the economically-priced labor offered by poorer countries. The poor countries are encouraged to get addicted to the inflow of manufactured goods from the developed countries. They are also encouraged to gorge themselves on borrowed capital from the rich countries, resulting in chronic strangulation in the debt trap. Yet, what they have to offer (labor) is devalued and rejected. All this is tantamount to a recipe for the perpetuation of poverty.

3. *Reforming the United Nations [18 July 1997; edited 2002]:*

We hear so much hue and cry about reforming the United Nations. The big western powers are particularly loud in this agitation, especially when the UN declines to rubber-stamp one of their imperial global adventures. How could one forget the scurrilous and persistent denigration of the UN in America when the UN begged to differ on the existence of weapons of mass destruction in Iraq? There were strident calls for reforming the UN to make it easier for powerful countries like the US to have their way. Of course, no apologies were forthcoming when it eventually turned out that the UN position on Iraq had been the correct one all along.

In all the talk, the pushers for the UN reform process have very carefully avoided any talk of reforming the veto power granted to a half dozen countries. Is it not obvious to them that the veto power is the most undemocratic principle in the whole system? An abhorrent undemocratic system that was set up in another age continues to be perpetuated, just because the powerful countries benefit from it. Is it not time to revisit and reform the veto system? I guess it is easy to champion democracy and reform only when it suits your cause.

4. *Arms development, proliferation, and dealing [14 December 2002].*

Today's Western powers, especially the US, are at the forefront of developing, stocking and threatening to use weapons of mass destruction, including nuclear weapons. Is it not clear that our possession of such weapons is the biggest incentive for others to try to acquire them? We've coaxed the world into showing that it is civilized by banning even the possession of chemical weapons (e.g. Sarin gas). So, there is already a precedent for asking everybody to refrain from making or possessing certain weapons. Why can this not be extended to nuclear weapons which are infinitely more lethal than chemical weapons? Is this perhaps a case of the powerful nations banning the possession of "poor people's" weapons of mass destruction, while those powerful nations continue to hoard the "rich people's" weapons of more massive destruction? Is this a case of hypocrisy that is gambling away the fate of humanity?

We are continually patrolling the world as the self-appointed Father Christmas, deciding who should or should not get the gift of being allowed to develop nuclear technology. India can get it but North Korea cannot. Israel can get it but Iran cannot. All the while, we are reluctant to reduce our own stockpiles of these weapons. We are even unwilling to put a stop to our further research, refinement and improvement in the lethality of such weapons. Where lies the morality in forcibly preventing others from acquiring a technology that we insist on flaunting? Is the hypocrisy not obvious?

Meanwhile, we are proliferating arms all over the world by being the world's biggest arms supplier by a wide margin. The mother of all arms proliferators, you might say. Just because it is good business, we deliver arms to more countries than any other nation on earth. The morality of the exercise begs in vain for consideration.

5. *Human rights [14 December 2002]*

For nearly the first 200 years of its existence, the US systematically and legislatively deprived a substantial proportion of its own citizens of basic human rights. It is only in the last 30 years that a semblance of redress has come to the situation of blacks, and even then, it's still a work in progress. In addition to slavery, long-practiced human rights abuses in US history include castrating and sterilizing your own citizens just because they are mentally handicapped, or you simply don't want certain sane people to reproduce (e.g. famous cases in North Carolina and Oregon). They include the practice of continuing to execute minors and mentally handicapped people for crimes committed. They also included the practice of deliberately infecting your own people (blacks) with syphilis to test out its effects, as in the Tuskegee studies from 1932-1972, where the US government deceived the victims into believing that they were receiving health benefits. The genocidal bounty-hunting of Native Americans in the early history of the US also fits in this category. Like the strangling fig that eventually kills off its host tree, the uninvited guests deliberately strove to decimate the Native Americans. Absolute decimation may not have been achieved, but the victim has been beaten into a comatose condition.

For a country that has been a crass human rights violator for most of its history, you would think that the US would be humble in its claim to be the world's bastion of human rights and freedom. On the contrary, the US has always been scathing in its castigation and punishment of countries that it declares to be in breach of human rights. Having crossed the bridge, albeit as a latecomer, the US arrogantly has little patience for stragglers or those who are still working out how to cross it. Given its own sordid history, a little less posturing and a little more humility or contrition might seem appropriate.

6. *Protectionism [14 December, 2002]*

The US, like many western countries, provides subsidies and protectionism to its producers and businesses (e.g. farmers, steel, etc.).

Many politicians burnish their credentials with how successful they have been in wresting substantial subsidies from the federal government for their constituents. They clamor for stiff tariffs to protect our heavy industries and agriculture. Yet, those same politicians cry from the rooftops about our being the perfect practitioner of free market systems. The glaring contradiction is enough to blind anybody. But not us. Not US.

To make matters worse, we pile pressure on other countries to remove the subsidies and protectionist tariffs that their producers enjoy. The case of farmers is particularly poignant and repugnant. In developed countries like the US and France, farmers enjoy huge subsidies which enable them to produce surpluses that are dumped on poorer countries, making the farmers in developing countries unable to compete. Yet, these developed countries, touting the need for a free market, insist that the poor countries must abolish subsidies for their own farmers as part the structural adjustment programs. Poor countries that refuse to remove subsidies and open up their markets are punished in various ways, including the denial of international development capital. It's a case of, "I will continue to subsidize my farmers, but will punish you if you subsidize yours. It's a free market for me to do as I wish, and to tell you how to behave." Free for some.

7. *Militarism [14 Dec, 2002]*

The US has established military bases and forces in some 100 countries around the world. By contrast, it is unthinkable for any one of those countries to have a military base in the US. The American populace and polity would not countenance it. Because of this imbalance, there's a creeping feeling among Americans that they own the world and that it is their duty to patrol it. The world is their oyster.

The imbalance also means that most Americans are unaware of how irritating it can be to have a foreign country's military base next to your hometown. They are surprised when citizens of hosting countries balk at harboring the US foreign bases in their cherished homeland. Why do they hate us so? Well, wonder no more and know that some of the answers lie in this kind of hypocrisy. Put yourself in their place and see how it feels. Remember that no nation has a monopoly on patriotism. For people in other nations, part of their expression of patriotic fervor is to oppose the existence of foreign bases in their homeland. That is their own brand of patriotism. Which American would not be similarly offended if foreign powers built and operated military bases in their home district?

Along the same lines, the US is eager to let its citizens command multi-national forces, but forbids any of its units to be commanded by a foreigner. Again, a hypocritical imbalance and asymmetry.

8. *Supporting Dictators while claiming to defend democracy [14 Dec, 2002]*

While touting itself as a defender of democracy around the world, the US has been very selective in such defense. The practice has been to support and prop up undemocratic regimes when it suits you, while conniving to dismantle democratic ones when it suits you. It seems that the guiding principle is not democracy, but crass opportunism.

Glaring historical examples of America propping up demonic regimes would include Franco in Spain, Batista in Cuba, Salazar in Portugal, minority rule in Bahrain, Apartheid in South Africa, Mobutu in Congo, the Sheiks in the Gulf, Smith in Rhodesia, Trujillo in the Dominican Republic, and Marcos in the Philippines. On the other hand, examples of our sustained subversion of democratically elected governments include Allende in Chile, Lumumba in Congo, Hamas in Palestine, Ortega in Nicaragua, Neto in Angola, Morsi in Egypt, Arbenz in Guatemala, Nkrumah in Ghana, and Chavez in Venezuela. In some cases, rebellious groups have been coaxed into the democratic process, in our hope that they will fail there; but then when they failed to fail, we've turned around to subvert and frustrate their democratic gains. This sets bad precedents. The list goes on to include outright invasion of countries with unfriendly governments, as can be exemplified by Grenada, Panama, and the Dominican Republic. In the choice between the demonic and the democratic, we've many times sided with the former. The self-appointed self-anointed global purveyor of freedom has often found itself dealing in a counterfeit version of the commodity. While insisting that the counterfeit is the real thing.

22

Recasting The American Dream:
Better to be loved than feared

__Context__: Written in Chambersburg, Pennsylvania, between 17 July and 12 October 2002, as the clouds were gathering for the Iraq War. Updated 10 February 2003.

I s it better to be feared than loved? Or vice versa? The Italian philosopher, Niccolo Machiavelli, pondered this question and concluded that it was better to be feared than loved, if you cannot be both. Of course, it is very rare to be both feared and loved. Indeed, fear is the antithesis of love in many situations. So, a choice has to be made between them.

Fear, unlike love, is often found in a relationship that is based on the domination of one by the other. Such an asymmetrical relationship can never attain an enduring stable equilibrium. Even the unstable equilibrium which it occasionally attains is only possible through constant or intermittent introduction of force into the system. The fear derived from force is what gives the system a semblance of equilibrium. The need for force never ends. This point has significant implications for "the world order" in today's world.

Nations cannot have it both ways in the choice between fear and love. The one demands an ever-increasing ratcheting up of the forces of coercion and warfare; the other demands humility, and a willingness, despite superior physical power, to share the responsibilities and rewards with fellow travelers in the little boat that we call Earth. The one holds the illusory promise of immediate dramatic positive results; the other gives a semblance of capitulation but holds the prospect of an enduring positive relationship, serviced with a minimum of tension, force, or coercion. The one is consistent with haughty unilateralism; the other engenders international cooperation.

A position of strength should not always lead to a position of arrogance. Indeed, in Christian theology, the ultimate position of strength (Godliness) was combined with unmitigated humility. Strength combined with arrogance is intoxicating to the strong as well as to the weak observers. The mix of strength and arrogance breeds resentment. Worse still, this combination provokes the weak to find ways to reduce the strength of the strong. Strength with humility, on the other hand, is more acceptable to the weaker beholder, who somehow feels invited to rally to further strengthen the strong.

Superpowers that have attained military and economic leadership of the world need to complement their status with *moral* leadership as well. The American dream is currently cast mainly in material and materialistic terms. The system is full of self-serving gimmickry intended to enrich the one (person or nation) while insidiously exploiting the other.

The American Dream needs to be recast in moral and moralistic terms. This is particularly needful in the area of dealings between nations and peoples. Moral leadership of the world, so far elusive, is what America should aspire to, if only to complement its economic and military power. Sages through the ages have taught us about the erosive potential (for nations) of moral bankruptcy and pride. These attributes formed the major focus in the Lamentations of Jeremiah for his ancient nation. Similarly, the hubris and moral decadence that brought down the Roman Empire represent more recent lessons for us all. Let the American dream include an ethical dimension as well. That is the only way to move from global dominance through fear to global leadership through love.

23

Apples Hang From Trees, Not From The Sky: Comment on the Green Party in America (2003)

__Context__: Written on 25 March 2003 in Chambersburg, PA, USA.

Apples do not hang from the sky. They hang from trees. So, to have an apple, you must first plant a tree and nurture it to maturity. Expecting an apple to hang from the sky is an unrealistic pie in the sky. A pipe dream.

The situation of the Green Party in the US is a poignant demonstration of this principle. The party has been contesting presidential elections for decades. Yet, it does not have even a congressman, a senator, a governor, or a big-city mayor. If the members' interest is only for publicity, that is fine. The presidential campaign certainly brings in publicity.

But I suspect that their interest goes beyond publicity. One hopes that their interest is for meaningful impact and lasting change. If so, then they need to focus their energies on getting a few lower-level political positions, around which and from which they can then build their national political ascendancy. They should borrow a leaf from green parties in Europe which have tried to build from the ground up in most cases. This has led to relatively greater political success, to the extent where, in some countries, the green party has been in national coalition governments, and has even produced a powerful foreign minister in Germany.

Expecting apples to hang from the sky is just as futile as building castles in the air. The sky is the limit, but you may have to wait an eternity to harvest apples hanging from it. Fruitful apples hang from planted, tended, nurtured, trees.

24

Choose Warlessness, Not War: The dynamics of War-Mongering

> *__Context__: This article was composed on various dates between Feb 24, 2000 and March 31, 2003. It started before the US embarked on the wars in Iraq and Afghanistan, but the thinking was fueled by the developments that led up to both wars, and the subsequent prosecution of the wars. The essay gives voice to my long-held view about wars, and about society's cavalier attitude to the role of war in human affairs.*

The next major evolutionary step for mankind will require a quantum leap. I don't expect us to grow wings and fly, or to be able to regrow lost limbs. The evolutionary step that I envisage will not even be physical. It will simply necessitate evolving beyond the propensity to use war as a means for settling matters.

An alien landing here from outer space might well marvel at how barbaric human beings are, given all the violence, destruction and dehumanization associated with warfare. It is amazing that human beings, who have now nearly invented how to create another human being, are still unable to invent a way to stop killing one another. It is a wonder that a species that has been able to send probes to outer space, is still unable to acquire the inner discipline needed to make warfare obsolete. As long as the basic animal instincts in humanity remain untamed, so long will this next evolutionary step continue to elude our species. Reining in the aggressive instinct, taming the human being, will probably be the last chapter in taming nature. It is the ultimate challenge. As human society continues to develop, there should perhaps be a new "civilization of love", a civilization that has progressed beyond war, and where the paradigm of *Warlessness* is the rule.

There are many factors militating against a warless civilization. These include the well-known factors such as the biological instinct for aggressiveness, as well as the economic benefits for warmongers. However, very little attention has been paid to several other insidious factors that make war so attractive, and the dream of warlessness that much harder to achieve. These factors include patriotic war-mongering, and the sanitization of war to make it seem like a normal human activity. These factors are discussed below.

Patriotic war-mongering

Suppose you have a son. Since he was born, you have been drilling into him the need to be honest. You've been telling him how opposed you are to stealing. Then suddenly, in his teenage years, he is caught stealing and is charged to court. On the day of the trial, you are there in court to support him. Weeks later, you hear your son telling his friends that his father supports stealing; after all, he was there in court to support him (son) who was charged with stealing.

This metaphor is analogous to the dilemma of those who oppose the hasty drive to war that our leaders are often guilty of. The war opponents can shout all they want in the lead-up to war, but once the war has started, their voice is muted by the need to show patriotic support for the troops. The war opponents are forced (some say, blackmailed) to change or hide their original positions for fear of being labeled anti-patriotic. They must now rally and show support, just as the father showed support in court for his son that was caught stealing. Opposing the war is equated with opposing the troops who are fighting it.

Ironically, the new willingness of former opponents to now "support" the war is factored into the opinion polls. Those who have always pushed for the war triumphantly point out that a high percentage of the population supports the war in progress. Once the shooting starts, a war whose antecedents were supported only by a minority, suddenly transmutes into a war that is supported by the majority.

This metamorphosis from an unpopular cause to a popular war has numerous unfortunate implications. For one, it makes it very easy for unpopular causes to be transformed into popular wars by over-ambitious leaders. Worse still, the leaders can afford to ignore public opinion in their drive towards war, confident in the fact that once the war starts, everybody supports it. Why waste time in the unpopular pre-war phases debating the justness of the cause, when you can move quickly to the actual war stage where your popularity ratings are assured? It is almost like the boy flagrantly ignoring his father's early advice to be honest, counting that his father will always be there to support him if he gets caught stealing. Just as the boy above cannot distinguish between his father's support for him as a person, and support for his cause (stealing), so some people cannot distinguish between support for the troops and disdain for the unjustness of the war. This situation encourages and rewards reckless behavior on the part of political leaders.

The grotesque nature of flippant and frivolous war-mongering goes even further. When, as in Iraq or Vietnam, the war is eventually acknowledged as unjust, how do you reverse the damage already done to human lives on our side: lives snuffed out in their youth; lives crumpled up just as they were beginning to flower; lives derailed into an abyss of unrelenting suffering? And on the other side, there's an even more damning panoply arraying the destruction of lives, of loves, and of livelihoods. No, the damage cannot be undone or even repaired; and very little attempt is made to do so. Even a formal apology for the bellicose blunder is not forthcoming from the lips of the proud perpetrators of the plunder. Each time, a lack of full accountability sows the seeds for impunity next time around.

The rules of War; the rules of what? – enter an Absurdity

Suppose somebody got up at a city council meeting and said, "Let us make rules by which people in this community will steal from one another." That sure would raise eyebrows and rouse any drowsy council members to attentiveness. I'm sure everybody present would consider it an absurd suggestion. Stealing is not an acceptable practice in this community; therefore, we do not make rules by which we should practice it. To make such rules would be an indirect way of permitting stealing to flourish, and regulating how we should behave when we are engaged in stealing. OK. A similar absurdity would arise if we made "rules" for murdering your neighbor, cheating at examinations, running red traffic lights, or shoplifting. In each case, it is equally absurd to make rules for carrying out activities that are not acceptable to the community in the first place. The only rule is that the activity should NOT occur at all. We do not need rules to regulate how we carry out an activity that should not be occurring in the first place.

If rules for stealing, cheating, raping, and murdering are absurd for a community, how did the community of nations come to adopt and accept something called "the rules of war"? Is this not an indirect legitimization of warfare in human affairs? As with stealing, should the only rule not simply be that this sort of activity is NOT acceptable, and we do not encourage people to carry it out by making rules on how to do it? "The rules of war" probably trivializes and legitimizes warfare, goading people on to practice warfare in the asinine belief that since there are rules for it, it must be a civilized activity. War must be seen for what it is: the ultimate expression of human depravity.

It is a fallacy to say that war cannot be eradicated because it derives from base human instincts. The project of human civilization is hugely dependent on the taming of man's biological instincts. The young man attracted to his neighbor's beautiful wife can long and pine away for years. But civilization prevents him from acting on his biological longing and dragging her off to bed. Rape has been made taboo by civilization. The same can be said of cannibalism, stealing, or even littering. If these human instincts can be made taboo, then why not warfare? Warfare is the most uncivilized manifestation of civilized man. Who says we cannot truly take our civilization beyond war by making war taboo and obsolete?

Sanitizing War

Our rulers go to great lengths to sanitize war to make it palatable for us. It's a bitter pill that's administered to us with a thick but odious sugar coating. In conspiracy with some of the mass media, the rulers do not even want us to see the gory details that war inevitably produces, because seeing them might make us more wary about recourse to war as a solution for human affairs. Even our own war dead are stealthily smuggled home to some remote air force base, and buried quietly, in order to insulate the populace from the reality that real people are really dying.

And what about the soldiers that survive the wars? Little publicity is given to the wretched lives that even the so-called surviving soldiers have ahead of them: years of incapacitation for the wounded; high risk of suicide for the traumatized; family destabilization for those inured to violence. Very little of these collateral effects are included when the statistics of a particular war are tallied. Many of the surviving soldiers are bedeviled with life-long strife. They would gladly trade their chest-full of gleaming medals for the normal quiet life they once knew. Of course, the authorities want us to see them all as heroes, which many of them may well be. Heroes deserving of praise and medals. But are they not, in truth, better described as victims? Victims of our appetite for war. Victims deserving of sympathy; more so if they had no choice but to fight (and suffer injury or death) in unjust or unpopular wars. Any leader who hastily embarks on an unjust war must bear moral responsibility for the suffering of these victims at home. Add to that the suffering of victims abroad, on the other side.

We are fed with images of veterans marching energetically in parades, with prominent chests, medals, flags, and attire. Patriotism at its finest. But for every day that they march, they suffer a hundred days wallowing in misery, out of the public eye. For every one that is marching, there are dozens of others crumpled up in a war-inflicted vegetative state in their lonely homes. The war mill that continuously mints these damaged veterans is operating full blast, continuously disgorging its bad coin. It continues to mint a currency that society is obliged to honor, but whose production is a manifestation of human malfeasance. The fewer the wars, the fewer the veterans, whether heroic or crumpled-up. The old adage about supporting the troops by bringing them home has often proved to be true in many instances through the ages.

The sanitized war is easier for us to live with, socially and politically. This is analogous to the practice where (unlike many other parts of the world) we Americans do not want to see the pig or rabbit carcass when we by our meat. Just give me the neatly packaged slab of chop. I do not want to be reminded that the slab of pork chop came from a living pig that was killed, skinned, and hung up. I do not care to know that my steak comes from a cow that was killed and quartered. Give me the "benefits" of war and spare me the horrendous specifics. Strip away the gory details and hand me the glory. I'm fine with the gory glory.

25

Gross Human Suffering (GHS):
The yardstick of all conflicts

Context: Written 29 March, 2003 in Chambersburg, PA, USA.

Where do you draw the line between "us" and "them"? Do you draw it at the surface of your own skin? Do you draw it at the door of your house to enclose only your family? Do you draw it at the city limits of your town, or at the boundary of your state? Do you draw it at the borders of your country, or at the limits of your race and culture? If there are so many possibilities in how you can draw this line, why then do so many people arbitrarily draw it at the border of their country?

The only truly non-arbitrary boundary for "us" is one that includes "them" as well – all of humanity. When theologians say that each of us is a "child of God", they are in effect affirming the oneness of the human family. They are saying that the definition of "us" must include everybody. No exceptions.

If somehow we are able to see "us" as embracing all of humanity, then there is a significant paradigm shift in how we perceive things. War, for example, becomes a much less facile recourse for settling human affairs. In that case, the cost of a war would be measured not so much in how many casualties our side suffers, but how many casualties humanity suffers. Not so much how relatives of casualties on our side are impacted, but how relatives of casualties on all sides are impacted. It is important to focus on the *Gross Human Suffering* (GHS), i.e. the summation for all sides, of all the dead, wounded, harassed, displaced, frightened, debased, and destroyed human lives.

When we add to the GHS, the frittering away of the earth's resources that occurs in warfare (expensive bombs, ammunition, planes, destroyed infrastructure, etc.), it becomes even more difficult to see how a positive net sum can be achieved.

Defining "us" to embrace all of humanity also forces us to rethink the concept of "enemy". If everybody is part of "us", then there should be no such thing as "enemy". As with "war", we should be striving to make the concept of "enemy" obsolete. Disagreements and differences can still exist, just as they do even in nuclear families. But the sorting out of such differences begins with the premise that these are "differences among us", and that our organic coherence remains intact while the differences are sorted out.

Unfortunately, there are people who see the existence of enemies as being essential for their own existence. I call these people the *enmity-profiteers*. They are particularly prominent in the political space, especially in the US. These are people who thrive on the fear created in the populace by the existence of enemies. They have learned to tap into profitable rich veins of fear. They will go to great lengths to ensure that enemies exist, and that we are seized with fear and trembling about the harm they are poised to do us.

Any country that opposes the hegemonic or imperialist tendencies of the US is immediately labeled as an enemy, and its leader is automatically reclassified as dictator. Friendly countries do not have sitting dictators, be they Marcos in the Philippines, Mobutu in Congo, Mubarak in Egypt, or the autocratic sheiks in the Persian/Arabian Gulf. But you remain a dictator/enemy if you're critical of the US, even if, like Chavez in Venezuela, you've had to fight and win multiple fiercely-contested presidential elections; and even if, like Putin in Russia, your approval rating is higher than that of the sitting US president.

Strangely, the obliging obsequious US populace and news media are only too willing to go along with the skewed and facile definition of enemy, as fed to them by the politicians. Countries that have never attacked or even threatened the US are consistently labeled as enemies both by the government and by the populace. The politicians need the fear engendered in the populace by this label, and will go to great lengths to stoke that fear. Allied to the politicians in this regard are some economic enmity-profiteers in the military-industrial complex; profiteers whose businesses thrive on the spoils of enmity. All this is aided by the ethos of duality in American culture: "If you're not with us, then you're against us."

26

Chauvinism Over The Top

Context: *Written 2 April, 2003 in Chambersburg, PA, USA.*

Let us suppose that you have a pot-luck dinner. Everybody brings a dish from their home and places it on the table at the dinner venue. Socialization continues for a while until suddenly, someone rings a hand bell for the dinner to commence. All attendees gather round the table. Rather than mixing the dishes, each person goes ahead and eats the dish that she brought. Nobody tastes the dishes of other people. What a shame that the opportunity for interactive sharing is squandered.

It is the same way that I see international sporting events where reporters are only interested in their own country's performance. They think that their compatriots back home are only interested in our (their) country's performance. They then go ahead and oblige. Watching or listening to some of the coverage (e.g. the Olympics), you would hardly know that there were dozens of other countries in the competition.

Unfortunately, this is a system that feeds on itself. The media provides the "patriotic" coverage that they think their citizens want; the citizens in turn begin to expect the "patriotic" coverage in future events. Where then will they get to know how citizens of other countries see and feel about what is going on? When you listen to or watch some media in the Olympic Games, for example, you would think that it was only their (our) country competing. All the highlights, coverage, replays, etc. are focused on our country's performance, with only perfunctory mention of the nearly 200 other competing nations. What is wrong with citizens of country A being interested in how countries B-Z perform?

This same phenomenon has even crept into the coverage of war, especially the Iraq war. Active interest and coverage stop with our own casualties, our own people held as prisoners of war, the impact on our lives, how we feel about what is going on, etc. Never mind how the civilians on the other side are coping: their casualties; their disrupted lives; their evidence of collateral damage; their double jeopardy of being politically impotent and physically devastated.

The phenomenon of getting fed with information related only to your country has inherent dangers. It results in people in different countries building up different and sometimes conflicting information packages. Opinions and views built on differing information packages are bound to differ. Tunnel vision sets in. Myopia rules. The overlap in their information packages continues to diminish, further accentuating differences in world view, and increasing the potential for conflict. Polarization results, with each side believing passionately that their opinion is the correct one. Tension builds up; the possibility of compromise disappears, and the lurch to war goes from possible to probable.

If all sides were able to continually share the same pool of information, the likelihood of polarization is very much reduced. The new world information highway (internet, blogs, etc.) may contribute to the commonality of shared information, but only if it can ensure that everybody has an equal opportunity to be heard, and that the information does not flow asymmetrically from the powerful to the weak.

The progressive speciation of mass media is another phenomenon that insidiously promotes the polarization of society. Liberals get all their news and opinion from liberal media; conservatives get all theirs from conservative media; religious people get all their information from religious stations, and so on; with very little overlap in what the various groups watch and hear. If you're interested only in sports, there's a channel to give you that round the clock to the exclusion of all else; and if within sports you only like golf, there's also a specialized channel for that. The isolation phenomenon exists even within the same family. The era of the entire family gathering around one TV to watch the same show is slowly vanishing. Now, there are enough TV and radio outlets in the home that parents and children hardly ever watch or listen to the same programs or stations.

The specialized media outlets are fully conscious of the kind of patronage they attract. Many of the outlets deliberately pander to their skewed clientele, providing them with news and opinion that are deliberately slanted in their direction. They create an echo-chamber into which they wall in their clients. With time, the phenomenon keeps feeding on itself and driving the clients to ever increasing narrowness in their views. Eventually, minor slants in what each group watches/hears have the cumulative centrifugal effect of creating major divergences of opinion and world view. The isolated pockets of listeners/viewers invariably drift in different directions in terms of their attitudes, beliefs, and judgments. Just as different species in biology arise due to isolation, so divergent poles of opinion develop due to failure to have enough common ground of shared viewing and listening. As each opinion or world view feeds on itself and hardens, the divergence and polarization of society continue to accelerate. The consequences for communal cohesion and world peace are huge.

SECTION B:

POEMS

[Philosophical; Occasion-marking; Tribute-rendering; Jocular]

1

Damaged Goods

Context: Written in 1997 while I was making a connection at the airport in Brisbane, Australia.

DAMAGED GOODS

Who, in all sincerity,
In all honesty and veracity
Can claim that their baggage is unblemished?
No!
On close examination
We're all, without exception,
Damaged goods.

2

Unsung Heroes

Context: In my dairy entries written on 19 July 1997, I stated that one of the enduring legacies of western culture is the indomitable spirit of their humanitarian agencies. In Bosnia, Rwanda, Chechnya, Cambodia, Haiti, or anywhere else where human suffering rears its head, they are there. No matter whether the suffering is man-made or natural, self-inflicted or brought on by other people. Even when the people they have come to help turn on them and attack them (as in Chechnya), they still persist and persevere. And yet, most of these people are professionals to whom a very comfortable life is available back in their home countries. Still, forsaking all, they trudge on in the name of humanity. Apart from western culture, I have yet to see any other culture on earth that has produced such a crop of self-denying, all-suffering, activists. Bravo to these "unsung heroes". Doctors Without Borders (Médecins Sans Frontières) exemplifies this ethos, and it has been my favorite charity for years. This poem is my expression of gratitude to them and similar organizations.

The poem was written on 8 February, 1995, while waiting for the airport bus at Inverness Court Hotel, London. It was originally dedicated to my son, Kenolisa.

in stealing. OK. A similar absurdity would arise if we made "rules" for murdering your neighbor, cheating at examinations, running red traffic lights, or shoplifting. In each case, it is equally absurd to make rules for carrying out activities that are not acceptable to the community in the first place. The only rule is that the activity should NOT occur at all. We do not need rules to regulate how we carry out an activity that should not be occurring in the first place.

If rules for stealing, cheating, raping, and murdering are absurd for a community, how did the community of nations come to adopt and accept something called "the rules of war"? Is this not an indirect legitimization of warfare in human affairs? As with stealing, should the only rule not simply be that this sort of activity is NOT acceptable, and we do not encourage people to carry it out by making rules on how to do it? "The rules of war" probably trivializes and legitimizes warfare, goading people on to practice warfare in the asinine belief that since there are rules for it, it must be a civilized activity. War must be seen for what it is: the ultimate expression of human depravity.

It is a fallacy to say that war cannot be eradicated because it derives from base human instincts. The project of human civilization is hugely dependent on the taming of man's biological instincts. The young man attracted to his neighbor's beautiful wife can long and pine away for years. But civilization prevents him from acting on his biological longing and dragging her off to bed. Rape has been made taboo by civilization. The same can be said of cannibalism, stealing, or even littering. If these human instincts can be made taboo, then why not warfare? Warfare is the most uncivilized manifestation of civilized man. Who says we cannot truly take our civilization beyond war by making war taboo and obsolete?

Sanitizing War

Our rulers go to great lengths to sanitize war to make it palatable for us. It's a bitter pill that's administered to us with a thick but odious sugar coating. In conspiracy with some of the mass media, the rulers do not even want us to see the gory details that war inevitably produces, because seeing them might make us more wary about recourse to war as a solution for human affairs. Even our own war dead are stealthily smuggled home to some remote air force base, and buried quietly, in order to insulate the populace from the reality that real people are really dying.

And what about the soldiers that survive the wars? Little publicity is given to the wretched lives that even the so-called surviving soldiers have ahead of them: years of incapacitation for the wounded; high risk of suicide for the traumatized; family destabilization for those inured to violence. Very little of these collateral effects are included when the statistics of a particular war are tallied. Many of the surviving soldiers are bedeviled with life-long strife. They would gladly trade their chest-full of gleaming medals for the normal quiet life they once knew. Of course, the authorities want us to see them all as heroes, which many of them may well be. Heroes deserving of praise and medals. But are they not, in truth, better described as victims? Victims of our appetite for war. Victims deserving of sympathy; more so if they had no choice but to fight (and suffer injury or death) in unjust or unpopular wars. Any leader who hastily embarks on an unjust war must bear moral responsibility for the suffering of these victims at home. Add to that the suffering of victims abroad, on the other side.

We are fed with images of veterans marching energetically in parades, with prominent chests, medals, flags, and attire. Patriotism at its finest. But for every day that they march, they suffer a hundred days wallowing in misery, out of the public eye. For every one that is marching, there are dozens of others crumpled up in a war-inflicted vegetative state in their lonely homes. The war mill that continuously mints these damaged veterans is operating full blast, continuously disgorging its bad coin. It continues to mint a currency that society is obliged to honor, but whose production is a manifestation of human malfeasance. The fewer the wars, the fewer the veterans, whether heroic or crumpled-up. The old adage about supporting the troops by bringing them home has often proved to be true in many instances through the ages.

The sanitized war is easier for us to live with, socially and politically. This is analogous to the practice where (unlike many other parts of the world) we Americans do not want to see the pig or rabbit carcass when we by our meat. Just give me the neatly packaged slab of chop. I do not want to be reminded that the slab of pork chop came from a living pig that was

UNSUNG HEROES

The storm gathers
The weapons of war are made ready
Compromise vanishes
Avarice reigns
The politicians hold sway
Reasonable voices are silenced
The world powers dither
Hither and thither
Reckoning their self-interests
Calculating their potential profits
Calibrating what they can gain.
The freeze sets in
Everybody's frozen into inaction…

Suddenly, the hot explosion
War!
Civil war!
Brother against brother
Friend against friend
Children suffer
Mothers suffer
All suffer.
The warlords now reign supreme
World powers uproot and flee
Posturing here, gesturing there
Talking everywhere
But doing nothing.

In the carnage and mayhem
In the butchery and confusion
In the anger and displacement
In the hunger and debasement
When all powerful persons have become beasts
Who is to cater to the human beings left?

The children
Their mothers
The displaced
The confused
The frightened
The sickly
The angry
The hungry
The civil wounded.

Now enter you my unsung heroes
With hearts larger than the world
With medicine that knows no frontiers
With compassion that knows no borders
With a passion that asks not why
With humaneness that embraces all of humanity

Forsaking the comforts of your comfortable homes
You stake your lives for the sake of lives.
The warlords love you but also hate you:
You clean up their mess to their delight;
But in vain they try to draw you to their cause.
They threaten you, they bully you,
But you smother their bombs in wads of cotton wool.
You douse their flames with tanks of drinking water
Filling empty stomachs with loaves of bread
Filling hollowed-out humans with loads of hope.

When at last the conflict has run its course
The beasts are exhausted, the humans decimated
The fled powers return with accolades
Bestowed here and there mostly on beasts
No one recalls your role in ensuring
That human beings did not vanish from the place.
My unsung heroes remain on song;
My unsung heroes remain unsung.

killed, skinned, and hung up. I do not care to know that my steak comes from a cow that was killed and quartered. Give me the "benefits" of war and spare me the horrendous specifics. Strip away the gory details and hand me the glory. I'm fine with the gory glory.

25

Gross Human Suffering (GHS):
The yardstick of all conflicts

__Context__: Written 29 March, 2003 in Chambersburg, PA, USA.

Where do you draw the line between "us" and "them"? Do you draw it at the surface of your own skin? Do you draw it at the door of your house to enclose only your family? Do you draw it at the city limits of your town, or at the boundary of your state? Do you draw it at the borders of your country, or at the limits of your race and culture? If there are so many possibilities in how you can draw this line, why then do so many people arbitrarily draw it at the border of their country?

The only truly non-arbitrary boundary for "us" is one that includes "them" as well – all of humanity. When theologians say that each of us is a "child of God", they are in effect affirming the oneness of the human family. They are saying that the definition of "us" must include everybody. No exceptions.

If somehow we are able to see "us" as embracing all of humanity, then there is a significant paradigm shift in how we perceive things. War, for example, becomes a much less facile recourse for settling human affairs. In that case, the cost of a war would be measured not so much in how many casualties our side suffers, but how many casualties humanity suffers. Not so much how relatives of casualties on our side are impacted, but how relatives of casualties on all sides are impacted. It is important to focus on the *Gross Human Suffering* (GHS), i.e. the summation for all sides,

3

Silence Has Spoken: Silence loaded with meaning

Context: The background to this poem lies in my scientific training which emphasized the use of the smallest number of words to say what you had to say. Written in September 2001 in Chambersburg, Pennsylvania, USA.

SILENCE HAS SPOKEN: Silence loaded with meaning

I find myself
Indulging in the exercise
Of concentrating linguistic meaning
Into the fewest possible words.
How much meaning, I wonder,
Can you pack into a single line of words,
Or into a single word,
Or even into a single alphabetical letter?
Of course, the ultimate in the frugal economy of words is:
How much dense concentrated meaning
Can you creatively craftily condense
Into a vacant blank page,
Into a wistful sigh,
Or even into
Silence
?
(Full stop)

4

Trustees Of The Earth

Context: *This poem was specially written and publicly read in October 2001, on the occasion of a presentation by me to the Board of Trustees of Wilson College, Chambersburg, Pennsylvania, USA. At that time, the author was professor and director of the Fulton Center for Sustainable Living (FCSL) at Wilson College.*

TRUSTEES OF THE EARTH

The forces of nature, our sacred trust,
The fortunes of nature, safeguard we must.
Living, consuming with responsibility,
In stewardship, for now and future humanity.
Investing in knowledge, in students empowered
Through FCSL, for future un-soured;
Like Wilson's Trustees Board, remember please,
We don't own the Earth, we're its trustees.

5

Believing In Sustainable Living

Context: Specially written and publicly read on May 31, 2001 on the occasion of Trustees and Donors unveiling signage at the Fulton Farm, Wilson College, Chambersburg, PA. At that time, the author was professor and director of the Fulton Center for Sustainable Living which included the Fulton Farm.

BELIEVING IN SUSTAINABLE LIVING

For those who give us strength today,
A word of thanks to you I say;
To Susan, Lucille, and all benefactors,
To Gwen, Lorna, Beate, all the actors
Whose thoughts and support permit us to dream,
Whose strength gives us strength and a head of steam.

Our eyes see far, but our reach is blunted;
Our dream is lofty, but our growth is stunted.
Are you with us, as we craft a new beginning?
Or will you wait until a tardy inning?

The task is there for you by the handful.
We're set for action; and wish you to be mindful,
That munificence to *Sustainable Giving*
Is the ultimate in *Sustainable Living.*

6

Vive Alive

Context: Written on 29 October 1998 in Rockville MD, USA, while visiting from Papua New Guinea.

VIVE ALIVE

However well you strenuously strive
To do all you can to stay alive
By the time you get to sixty-five
Age insidiously starts to contrive
To deprive you of your hard-earned vive.
At this stage, you're unable to thrive;
It's a dire struggle just to survive.

7

The Day Is Marked

Context: This very personal poem marks some significant dates for me and my family. It was written in Lae, Papua New Guinea, on 7 March, 1994, the first anniversary of an armed robbery attack at my home in Owerri, Nigeria. April 1 marks my involvement in a horrendous car accident. Of the joyful pair of dates, April 15 was my wedding anniversary and May 23 is my birthday.

THE DAY IS MARKED

Four dates of destiny, four dates with destiny surely,
Two like winter sorely, two in spring purely,
Two in Lent, and two in Easter-tide,
Two of suffering, and two of joy and pride.
March seven and first April, the pair of despair,
April fifteen and twenty-third May form the joyful pair.
For all of them, the pleasing and the hateful,
To God Almighty, I am most grateful.

8

Thomas Evans Ode

Context: Part of a message sent to the Evans family on hearing of the passing of Thomas Evans, May 25, 2001. The Evans family have remained life-long friends, having initially served as my second family during my student years at the University of California, Davis.

ODE TO THOMAS EVANS

We share the loss of a great man!
We share the grief of the moment.
But we also share the gift
Of having known him;
Of having learned from him;
Of having loved him;
Of having been loved by him.
It was a great life which gave life to all our lives.

9

You Made My Day

Context: This was specially written as a thank-you note sent on August 11, 2001 to a friend who had hosted me to dinner the night before.

YOU MADE MY DAY.

You made my day, you made my spirits soar,
Superb cuisine, the company the more;
Much fun for me, certainly worth repeating.
For you, I hope it was a worthy meeting.
And through the silence (ah Silence!), if I may,
I lean over, whisper: *Thanks for the day.*

10

Limericks

Context: *These limericks, each verse a stand-alone item, were written on various dates between 2002 and 2005. With my children, relatives, hometown (Ukala), and kindred (Umusizor) as objects, the limericks are mostly jocular jibes and jabs at the jugular.*

LIMERICKS

There was a young man from Ukala
Some six feet tall, maybe taller
His favourite food
When in a good mood
Was pounded yam with *ofe nsala*

Another young guy from Ukala
Had eyes each of a different color
Believe me it's true
Would I lie to you?
I swear it in the name of Allah!

There is a man of Umusizor
Whose front tooth's a monstrous incisor
It functions, mind you
For biting to chew
It's indeed a sharp dental scissor

There is this cool dude from Ukala
Whose stories were always a thrilla
They called him Abenja
Can handle all danger
When he is around, no *wahala*

This next story's mostly pertaining
To Philip with tales entertaining
Makes you laugh all night
Gripping you with fright
The king of fable's truly reigning

This fellow that we all call Sunny
His tales were quite tall and quite funny
Such tales electronic
Manifestly seismic
Are every bit sure worth the money

An UMOC member called Bangumba
Has his thighs full-packed just like lumber
He lifts heavy weight
Be advised, dear mate
If he asks to wrestle, just *si "mba"*

An Ukala lad named Baabundo
With whom I played ball near the window
When the game got tough
He tackled me rough
Then bent over *bia si mu "ndo!"*

That lass called Ebele's a marvel
With passion for consuming novel
Coiled up in a corner
Damning *onye obuna*
She'd read even when on a travel

135

Kiki, a girl we all admire
Does sports as if she is on fire
Do not rub her wrongly
She'll push back quite strongly
Sucking her tongue as pacifier

I ask you how, and you ask me why
The mystery stays until we both die.
Baby coins a word
That none's ever heard
Is there meaning to the word *tankwuai*?

Nice Ukala girl named Malije
She talks like she's some kind of DJ
You can truly tell
She is smart as hell
She dresses like she is from Fiji

A wily young priest by name Cosmas
Passed round some good grass during high mass
Bishop got to know
Th'eucharistic show
Banned Cosmas from mass until Christmas

11

The Stench Of Cash: Oh, have I got money for you?

Context: There are billions of stars in our Milky Way galaxy, many of them with numerous planets orbiting around them. Then there are billions of galaxies in our known universe. So, there are at least one billion times one billion heavenly bodies in our cosmos. Easy to say, isn't it? But have you ever stopped to ponder how big a number one billion is? This poem helps you to contemplate the sheer enormity of the billion, a word that should not be said lightly. The poem is also a light-hearted mathematical parody on the philosophy and ultimate futility of unfathomable riches. This was written in May 2006 in Springfield, Missouri.

THE STENCH OF CASH: Oh, have I got money for you?

"So you want money," you said to me.
"I do, I do," was my urgent plea.
"How much?" you asked, "No need to be so shy."
"Plenty of it; plenty," was my reply.
"Just how plenty?" was then your next big query.
"Very plenty," I said in a great hurry;
"I think it will just simplify my life,
Make life worthwhile and take away all strife."

You said you will be good and give me money,
But on one term which might seem a bit funny:
I must count it all before I start to spend.
I say, "No worries, you will become my friend.
Just bring the cash in any good amount.
Counting's a chore I can quite well surmount."

"Here's the money," you said. "Now test your skills;
Ten billion bucks all in one-dollar bills.
The secret of the real exact amount
Will be confirmed after you've done the count.
I hope your zeal for money's not diminished.
So, start counting and tell me when you've finished."

Excited by so much loot to be reckoned,
I start to count, about two notes per second.
After the first flurry of jubilation,
Realism comes, I stop for contemplation.
Use calculator to figure in a dash
How long it'll take to count up all this cash.
I punch the keys and do the calculating
But can't believe the answer that I'm getting.
I sum again, but get the same absurdity:
One hundred fifty, the years to count the booty.
Even suppose I live that long, in health,
What time is left to enjoy all this wealth?

12

Mr. Nameless Laments At
The Soup Kitchen

Context: _This poem was commenced on Christmas Day,
2001 in Chambersburg, PA, USA. Earlier in the day, I
had gone to assist the Salvation Army serve dinners to some
homeless and destitute people. It was quite a collection of
otherwise capable persons, but who somehow must have been
down on their luck. Some were probably victims of drug
abuse._

_The first two persons I served were two young white men
in their early 20's. One was of slight build and blonde hair
(Jeremy) and the other taller with dark hair (Tom). Jeremy
later requested seconds, which I fetched for him. I asked if
he had received any gift from the pile of gifts in the hall. He
said yes. He got one. He would reserve it for his girlfriend.
What of himself? None yet. So I went and got one for him.
Some 25 minutes later, Jeremy sought me out in the corner
where I was in the crowded hall. He had come to say thank
you, Merry Christmas, and goodbye. He was leaving. Even
though he was down on his luck, I saw a lot of decency and
humanity in this man. The considerate decency that had
prompted him to reserve the first gift for his girlfriend, the
same decency had moved him to shuffle through the crowd to
find me to express his gratitude. The hard times that drove
him to eat at this soup kitchen had not driven away his sense
of humanity. Tom had finished and left earlier._

One tall middle-aged (40-50's), toothless man, also white, sat at the end of the back table. He looked much battered, wore scruffy brown work overalls, and ate quite a bit. He cut the classical figure of the hungry being fed. He served as the inspiration for the poem below. This poem is dedicated to him. My experience was similar at the Thanksgiving Holiday in 2002, leading me to re-visit and edit the poem on 27 November 2002.

MR. NAMELESS LAMENTS AT THE SOUP KITCHEN

I had hoped for better in life but have had to settle for this,
I have seen much better in life, I have seen happiness and bliss.
But the vision soured and my luck ran out
My dreams went bust and I was put to rout.

Take me, hold me, clothe me, lead me,
Move me, nurse me, warm me, feed me.

I still hope for better, but now I dare not hope
But in you and Providence to help me cope
With pain and fears and what is left of life,
To ease my loss and minimize the strife.
My life has been so deftly garnished with sorrow
But I live on, in hope of better morrow.

13

The Public Auction

Context: Written in 2002 in Chambersburg, Pennsylvania, this is a tribute to all persons who battle to reduce the level of corruption in society.

THE PUBLIC AUCTION

To you that bear the scars of war
Wounded by greed and graft and more
To you that strive for conscience clear
Who dare to speak without much fear
Safeguard, I say, your souls from vile seduction
While most sell theirs in shameful public auction.

14

Too Proud To Talk: Let's talk!

Context: This piece was written in 2012.

The US and some other countries arrogantly refuse to talk to nations that disagree with them, even when such nations are eager to talk. Does having different views not accentuate the need to talk and dialog? Is talking to those with whom you disagree not more compelling than talking with your friends? In what situation is there a greater need to talk than when you have enemies that disagree with you? Who, I wonder, has the moral high ground: the enemy who is willing to talk despite our differences, or we who refuse to talk because of our differences? Talking or communicating should never be seen as a favor being done by one side to the other. If you cannot talk to your adversaries, then all your views reflect reinforcing resonations from the echo-chamber of your friends. Such self-defeating hubris deprives you of the opportunity to more fully understand your adversaries and yourself. We must remember that Communication is the stream that nourishes the tree of Understanding. Communication flow helps Understanding grow.

<u>TOO PROUD TO TALK: Let's talk!</u>

You think you're an angel, you think I'm the devil,
So you refuse to talk to me, even though I'm eager to talk to you.
You contemn me, then condemn me.
Let's talk.
Let's communicate.
If you can convince me that you are the angel that you claim to be,
I can convince you that I am not the devil that you say I am.
Let's talk.

15

The Transgressor's Shield:
Advice for the prodigal son

Context: Written in April 2006 in Springfield, Missouri, USA. It's construed as advice from a parent to an adolescent child going off to college.

THE TRANSGRESSOR'S SHIELD: Advice for the prodigal son

Be good, be good, you hear me say,
Be good and don't you go astray.
Do what is right
With all your might,
Fight a fair fight
What e'er your plight.
But then you ask: what should you do
When being good just eludes you?

I say to you, when in such situation
Do all you can to overcome temptation.
But above all do not compound the badness
With caution lost; *that* multiplies your sadness.
Be warned, I say, the sin of not being good
Is amplified when you are also slipshod.
From sages all we're bound to hear the earful:
If you cannot be good, try to be careful.

16

Affluenza

Context: Written in May 2014.

AFFLUENZA

Affluenza says to buy and buy
And pile purchases to the sky.
The way that we plan it
Much degrades our planet
Doing us grave harm by and by.

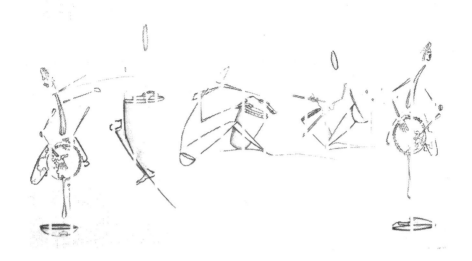

SECTION C:

RANDOM 'RITINGS, RANTINGS, AND RAVES

** *Fleeing from a weeping, vanishing, land mass: Perspective on African refugees* [Written 18 July 1997]

Africa entered the second half of the 20th century brimming with hope for the forthcoming emancipation from colonialism, and the attendant spurt in development. Political independence was seen as a harbinger of peace, progress, prosperity, and plenitude. Hope reigned supreme.

By the end of the century, all that hope had vanished into a thin air of despair. One of the most significant global developments in the past 50 years has been the transformation of Africa from a virile, agile, hopeful giant into a lethargic, lumbering invalid. A weakling wearily wallowing in wanton misery. Despite its land mass, Africa has continued to attenuate in quantity and quality in the world's consciousness. It is in the throes of evanescence, virtually vanishing before our very eyes like a magician's handkerchief.

How often have we seen global TV stations that comfortably leave out Africa in their live regional presentations? It is now safe to ignore Africa when many positive things are being discussed. But not when we come to poverty, disease, and war. The continent has manifested more than its fair share of these negatives, and few people can be blamed for associating these ills with Africa. One by-product of these strife situations is that Africa has generated large numbers of internal and external refugees. With refugees streaming out of a bleeding Africa, the world's bandage of patience is starting to fray. It might be helpful for us to pause and get some perspective on this flood of refugees from Africa.

Where would Europe be without an outlet for its population in the past half-millennium? Over the centuries, Europe has been very fortunate in having outlets by which its population could escape upheavals. For all its positive contributions to humanity, Europe has been the source of some of the greatest human scourges of the last two centuries: Colonialism, industrial-scale Slavery, Nazism, orthodox Communism and, vicariously, Apartheid. Add to these, their share of catastrophes that have also occurred in other parts of the world: plagues, famine, religious persecution, civil wars, etc. Each time a major upheaval occurred, a significant proportion of the European population found other parts of the world to which they could readily migrate. Such places included North America, South

America, Australia, Southern Africa, New Zealand, etc. Today there are more people of European stock outside Europe than in Europe. The upheavals that caused the migrations included religious persecution (e.g. Quakers to North America); famine (Irish to North America); wars (e.g. World Wars 1 and 2); political/social persecution (European Jews to various continents); and civil criminality (British prisoners to Australia). I wonder what Europe would have done and how it would have coped if it did not have all these places to relieve its population pressures.

Today, it is Africa that is undergoing the most serious upheavals. Unfortunately, there is nowhere to go. Its population is condemned to sitting it out and stewing in the upheavals. How lucky Europe was! But we should also keep a decent perspective on those who are not so lucky now. The cloudy image of refugees/migrants from Africa, especially in Europe, should be seen against the perspective of Europe whose own refugees over the centuries found welcome in other lands.

** *Important things first* [26 February 2006]

If you put the number 1 first, any zeros you add after it simply serve to increase the value. But if you put the zeros before the 1 (as in a decimal), the more zeros you put, the less the value. The lesson in this original metaphor is that we should seek the important things first, and add on the fluff later; not the other way around.

** *E-Max, the Effort Maximization Philosophy* [June 2013]

A philosophy which has guided me throughout my life is one that I can refer to as the *Effort Maximization* philosophy (*E-Max* for short). Let me try to explain it. In life, there are factors that are within your control and those that are beyond your control. The amount of *effort* (or input) you commit into each life situation is something you can increase or decrease at will, i.e. something you can control. On the other hand, the *results* (or outcomes) that emanate from the effort are much less controllable by you, because external uncontrollable factors could be at play. A definite path to happiness is to make sure you maximize the aspects that you can control. You do this by ensuring that your effort is always at its peak, and that you are doing your best at any given time. Once you have done that, the results (the uncontrollable aspects) can fall as they may, determined by other people or external circumstances.

It's like what happens when you approach a slot machine with your 25-cent coin. You put in your coin, it rattles through the system, and nothing happens. Another guy is sitting next to you playing another machine. He puts in his equally-denominated 25-cent coin. It rattles through the system, and suddenly, all hell breaks loose. Bells are ringing, lights are flashing. He's won the jackpot, and his gleaming winnings are pouring out of the spout in the machine. You look across to him with mixed feelings. His effort and input were exactly the same as yours; but the results were totally different. External factors have intervened. Should you now blame yourself for the way things turned out? Certainly not. As long as you have done your best in the first instance (earning and playing the coin), your happiness should not be disrupted or compromised by how the results turn out. You are at peace with yourself and can sleep easy at night, knowing that you have done all that you could have done. That, to me, is the philosophical basis of putting in your best effort at all times. The Effort Maximization philosophy. *E-max* not only improves the likelihood of a good result, but it also guarantees your happiness in the event of a bad result.

** *Your kindness is killing me; but thanks for the bad job* [2001]

So, your best friend Mary is a tailor or seamstress. You know she's not the best tailor in town, but you think she's pretty good all the same. You've recently told her about the several yards of expensive cloth that you bought with the intention of making a beautiful dress for yourself. You were still contemplating the high cost of having the dress made by the much better tailor across town. Then, in her kindness as a friend, and much to your relief, Mary offered to spare you the expense by making the dress for you free of charge. You gleefully accepted her offer.

Three weeks later, she delivered the finished dress to you, gushing about how beautiful she thought the dress looked. Much to your embarrassment, the final product comes across to you as awful, something you're not likely to want to wear to anywhere. As you ponder the situation, what sentiment comes to the fore? Is it anger with frustration at the lousy outcome and the waste of your beautiful cloth material? Or is it gratitude to Mary for the good gesture of offering to make the dress for free? Is it ire at the backfire or amity for the charity; frustration or appreciation? Which?

This situation is similar to the teenage boy who accepts a free haircut from his amateur barber cousin, but who winds up looking terrible afterwards. How does he get himself to be grateful for the dreadful haircut? Should the goodness of the intent overwhelm the badness of the outcome? Or vice versa?

** *Philosophical dilemma for change agents* [21 June 2003]

There is a dilemma that change agents often have to face. If your long-term goal is 100% change in 100% of the people, what do you strive for in the short term? Do you aim for:

5% change in 100% of the people

OR

100% change in 5% of the people?

I seem to prefer the former. If you take the change towards environmental sustainability as an example, it is better to have the entire population embracing it and practicing it, even if only to a small degree. The 5% change in 100% of the population enables the entire population to change in lockstep. It is also more sustainable since everybody is involved in the change. This seems more desirable than the opposite situation where a small cadre of devotees embraces change to the limit (100%), undertaking a lifestyle that the rest of the population see as distant. This option results in societal polarization, which in itself may produce political resistance that could threaten the change in question.

** *The Abortion decision* [9 March 2006]

Should the decision to abort a baby, be the sole prerogative of the woman? What if the father conscientiously believes and says, "That's also my baby you are killing." Now let's look at several possible scenarios:

- If both father and mother agree to keep the child – their joint will prevails. No debate there.
- If both agree to abort the child – their joint will also prevails, subject to the legality of abortion where they live.

- If the father wants to abort, but the mother does not – it is unlikely that any jurisdiction will force the woman to submit herself for an abortion against her will. She has a de facto veto.
- If the mother wants an abortion, but the father objects in conscience to the "killing" of his baby. This is the scenario that raises all kinds of questions and dilemmas. Do you grant the woman a veto, and proceed to "kill" the baby despite the father's objections? Or do you compel the woman to bear and deliver a child she does not want?

Maybe some way could be found to integrate the father's opinion into the abortion debate, especially in consensual or marital situations. Since procreation remains a joint responsibility of man and woman to society, it seems fair that neither of them should monopolize decision-making in the matter. Exceptions should of course be made for irregular situations, such as rape or incest. In such cases, the woman's veto on the baby's fate seems unquestionable.

** *Mediator's risk* [15 August 1997]

One of the risks you take when you step in to sort out a dispute is that stray punches, intended for the opponent, may land on you. In some cases, punches might in fact be aimed at you. This is true literally as well as figuratively. One or both antagonists may make it part of their strategy to draw you into becoming a disputant. You, the honest broker, now become an issue in the matter. I suspect that the side with a weaker case is more prone to this temptation of drawing the arbitrator into the dispute. It provides welcome distraction from the real issues. A good conflict "resolver" must find ways to avoid becoming an issue in the conflict. This is true in all situations, from interpersonal disputes all the way to disagreements between nations.

A corollary of this is that third parties should resist the temptation of hastily jumping into disputes on one side or the other. Once you take sides, it immediately rules you out of the pool of potential arbitrators. World powers, whose arbitration potential is huge, should be particularly wary about foreclosing their arbitration role by hastily taking sides. It's a mistake that many of them have made over and over again.

** *Tensions in nations* [16 August 1997]

In many modern nations, there are three kinds of tensions that one can see, among others:

> Individual Rights vs. Society Group Rights
> Freedom of the individual vs. Order in society
> Development vs. Democracy

History is replete with societies and nations that have selected various combinations from this menu of choices. Even today, the character of each nation is determined by the choices it makes from the menu.

** *Competition, Consumption, and Growth*
[16 August 1997 to 7 January, 2002]

There has to be something fundamentally suspicious about a system – any system – that relies primarily on the basest human instincts: one that relies on competition rather than co-operation; on consumption rather than frugality; on exploitation rather than conservation. I wonder how global capitalism stands up when measured by this yardstick. When things get tough and the economy is unsteady, it somehow goes against your natural instinct to be told to go out and spend, go out and consume in order to prop up the economy. Somehow, your natural instinct tells you that hard times are times for you to economize, spend less, and consume less. Yet capitalism urges the opposite.

It appears that the capitalist system is crucially dependent on a perpetual increase in economic consumption. Through the magic of credit, today you manage to consume tomorrow's expected earnings; tomorrow you consume next week's earnings; next week you consume next month's earnings; next month you consume next year's earnings. And so on. Eating off the future with a voracious appetite; eating up the future with reckless abandon.

But a perpetual increase in consumption can only be sustained with perpetual economic growth. We take a bite out of the future in the expectation that economic growth will heal the wound before the future arrives. As long as we are consuming the future through gratuitous credit, as long as there is increasing appetite for goods and services to maintain each individual, so long will there be a requirement for perpetual economic growth. One outcome of this is that if economic growth for some reason stalls, the system unravels. There is no way to fill the gaping hole that has already been gauged into the body of the future through wanton credit-driven consumption. Another corollary is that if we could manage to stabilize our appetite for increasing goods/services, and minimize our appetite for consuming the future, then the necessity for perpetual economic growth would have been avoided. We would have freed ourselves from an ever-whirling treadmill.

** *Are Hate and Love both burdens?* [3 September 2000]

Love is best when shared. Hate is worst when shared. Hate is a burden on the hater and we're advised not to carry it around. In a slightly different sense, I wonder if love is not also some sort of burden. The mutual obligations expected and entered into in a love relationship certainly imply a sort of burden on each side. The difference seems to be that the love burden is carried around with a grin, while the hate burden is carried around with chagrin.

** *Good and Bad exist in all societies* [15 February, 2003]

Point to something good or something bad in other societies, and I can show you an equivalent good or bad in our own society. Once we realize this point, it is much easier to understand how very similar various societies are. There is no such thing as our being all good and they being all bad.

Some might even argue that good and bad exist simultaneously in any individual. The aspect that gains prominence at any given time is dependent on the prevailing environment, influences, and circumstances. The same could even be said of social and economic movements including capitalism, socialism, and democracy. Beneath and beyond the propagandist balderdash of each such movement, there lurks the potential to gravitate towards malignancy and malfeasance. This means that none of such movements is pure or absolute. Instead, there are many species within each such movement, depending on the degree to which good and bad manifest themselves. Ultimately, though, the foibles of human nature take over. Like a crystal growing in a saturated solution, more power accrues to those who are already powerful, and more wealth accrues to those already wealthy. The propagandists wind up becoming the monsters that they preached against and supplanted. George Orwell's *Animal Farm* demonstrates this phenomenon very clearly.

*******Age as the immutable determinant*** [19 January, 1999]

Age is the immutable, intervention-neutral, point of reference between two persons. Today, you can be slimmer than I am, and tomorrow I will be slimmer than you. The same can be said of health, wisdom, wealth, fatness, tallness, etc. Either by nature or by human intervention, the places can be switched. But once I am older than you, that is fixed for ever. No natural or human intervention can change our relative positions. It is intervention-neutral. Is it any wonder then that so many traditional societies rely on age as a determinant of hierarchy?

** *Excess baggage in social/religious movements*
[10 January, 1999 and 14 April, 2002]

Suppose somebody you trust puts something in your mouth and says you have to eat it. It turns out to be a peanut with the shell on it. You oblige and begin to chew. But the material is hard to chew and swallow because of the shell. The kernel (the nutritious part) is there alright, but the shell makes it hard to swallow any part of the material, even the nutritious part. The shell is like excess baggage which masks and debases the essential part. Ultimately, you give up and spit out the entire thing, including the nutritious part. The presence of the chaff has adversely determined the fate of the nutritious part. Now, consider if the same person you trust puts a peanut without the shell in your mouth. You have no problem chewing and swallowing it. It is easier to chew, easier to swallow, and easier to digest. There is less likelihood that you will spit it out.

Social/religious movements have a lesson to learn from this metaphor. They should be wary of unnecessary philosophical excess baggage which ultimately tends to weigh them down and sink them. For example, orthodox communism could well have thrived and projected its virtues without the excess baggage of atheism. Similarly, Roman Catholicism could well have done without the doctrine of the Immaculate Conception, or the insistence on priestly celibacy. So could capitalism have done without the brigandage of the multi-national corporations. These bits of excess baggage repulse potential adherents who could easily have embraced the core principles of the movements. The excess baggage puts the movements at greater risk of being spat out and rejected. Stripping off the unnecessary baggage improves the palatability and acceptability of what is left. Just like removing the shell before putting the peanut in the mouth.

** *The perfect pacifist position* [30 May 2002]

When you roll yourself into a ball, people may be able to kick you around, but one thing they cannot do is break you in two. The ball position must, figuratively, be the ultimate pacifist position.

** <u>*All*</u> *the straws break the camel's back* [19 January 2000]

When the straws break the camel's back, we always say it was the last straw that did it. But this last straw is just as light (or as heavy) as each of the thousands of straws that went before it in the load. So, when the last straw goes onto the load, all the other straws have to take combined responsibility for breaking the camel's back. Lesson? When laying on all the other straws, be just as careful as you will be when you lay the last one. Each of them is a contributor to the breaking of the camel's back.

** *The silver lining* [21 January, 2000]

However cloudy it may be down here, remember that the sun is shining up there above the clouds. This happens literally, like when you take off from a cloudy airport and ascend above the clouds. You find that despite the darkness and gloom all around the airport precincts, there is bright sunlight up above. Figuratively, we can say that over all our cloudy earthly problems, the grace of God is there above smiling on us. The clouds have a silver lining.

** *Few friends, few enemies* [30 May, 2000]

I find that I have fewer friends than most people; but also, I like to believe that I have fewer enemies than most people. The vast majority of people I know are neither friends nor enemies. Which is better: having many friends and many enemies, or having few friends and few enemies?

** *Genetic Chauvinism* [3 June 2000]

When an adolescent male lion stages a coup and takes over a pride of lionesses, it does three remarkable things: it drives away the previous patriarch dominant male; it takes over the lionesses; and it kills all young cubs sired by the previous dominant male.

This last item is an extremely curious case of infanticide. It ensures that the lionesses come on heat (become sexually receptive) earlier than if they have young suckling cubs. At the genetic level, it ensures that it is the genes of the new male (not those of the old) that survive and perpetuate. A similar thing has been observed in some insects (e.g. dragon flies) where the sperm of a previous coition is actually flushed out by a male, before it inserts its own. Many other instances of what I might call genetic chauvinism exist in nature. Is there any element of this behavior in humans e.g. in second marriage situations? I wonder.

** *Nuclear annihilation* [10 June, 2000; edited 2014]

When nuclear annihilation comes, the only thing more eerie than flattened city houses will be cities with intact houses but no humans. The smart-killing neutron bomb will see to that. The nuclear disaster zones in Chernobyl and Fukushima have given humanity a foretaste of how scarily spooky such places can be.

** *Banking at church* [10 June, 2000]

The church is like a bank. Most people go there to deposit the imponderables which they encounter in their daily lives, and to withdraw the blessings and inspiration which they need to carry on.

** *The coin and the sphere* [3 January 2001]

Is it not incongruous when some supercilious western societies see everything in the two-sided way they see a coin? It is head or tail; black or white; good or evil; us or them; friend or enemy, etc. It's a culture dominated by duplicity in duality. There are few intermediate positions, few transitional sides. May we be reminded that the earth, our ultimate home, does not have two flat opposing sides? Instead, it is a sphere, in which transition from one side to the next is ever so gradual, ever so imperceptible.

Similarly, one often sees media outlets in America burnishing their sense of balance by featuring a Republican and a Democrat to discuss most issues, even foreign issues. It is the same bipolar view of things that fosters this habit. They forget (or ignore the fact) that the views of these two parties may both be on the fringe of the global universe of views on the matter at hand. This is likely to be most glaring when foreign issues are discussed.

Metaphorically, it is only in the situation of a straight line joining two points that you can conceivably achieve balance by applying weights at the two points. For a multi-point polygon, applying weights to two contiguous points only leads to a loss of balance, and greater instability. Things get tilted.

** *Leader <u>should</u> be close enough to be followed* [30 July, 2001]

When you are leading a child through a strange forest, you stay ahead and the child follows a few steps behind. But you do not go too far ahead. Why? If you do, the child loses your trail and gets lost.

So it is with advocacy groups (e.g. the environmental movement). The movement's leaders, even if they see far ahead, must not go so far ahead of the masses as to evoke a disconnect and possible opposition. This happens in many cases, and often leads to suspicion and resistance. Human nature is such that when you set the bar too high, most people are tempted to simply walk under it. When the leader is too far ahead, people despair and lose the zeal to follow. Educating and enlightening the masses often helps them to stay close, just behind the leaders.

Continuing with the original metaphor, you keep leading the child through the strange forest until you both emerge into a clear open road. You can now let the child walk ahead of you and you follow, keeping an eye on the child. Your places can now be reversed.

** *Leadership positions in Academia* [3 July 2007]

In academia, one often hears this sort of talk. Professor Jones says, "I love my teaching so much that I could never get myself to be a department head or dean." Professor Smith follows with, "I love my research so much that ….." I'm sure a similar positioning can be found in other professions. Such people see the department head and dean as being less enamored with teaching and research; that, they reason, must be why they accepted these leadership/administration positions.

Now, let's look at a metaphor. Mr. A loves granola. He eats it whenever he can, and will do all he can to have access to it. But that's as far as it goes. Mr. B loves granola too; but after enjoying it for some years, he decided to encourage others to enjoy it as well. He sets up a factory, produces plenty of granola there, and makes it available for others to enjoy. So, who loves granola more, Mr. A or Mr. B? I would say Mr. B. He has shown a higher order of love of granola than Mr. A. Moreover, Mr. B's love for granola is less focused on himself; it is indeed less selfish.

So when professors go about taunting their love for teaching or research as reasons for not offering themselves for academic leadership in these areas, they had better comprehend the full gravity of what they are saying. The leadership position provides exponentially greater opportunities to promote the love of teaching and research among many other colleagues, in addition to oneself. It is a higher order of love that also happens to be less selfish.

** *Loyalty* [17 July 1999]

Loyalty should not necessarily be a devotion to a physical person or entity. Instead, it should be targeted at a more fundamental level; at the level of the admirable ideas, principles, ideals, and characteristics which that person manifests. Once loyalty is keyed on these basic factors, it is not likely to be wavering or evanescent, so long as the object of the loyalty retains their original characteristics. If the object of loyalty jettisons the characteristics that initially attracted the loyalty, then the loyalty could justifiably remain with the jettisoned characteristics and migrate away from the original individual/entity.

This principle has special resonance in the field of international relations. The US and other nations sometimes adopt the flawed principle: they are our friends, therefore they are right. Rightness is preposterously made subordinate to friendship. A more justifiable principle should be: they are right, therefore they are our friends. This shows that the more fundamental attachment is to rightness, and that friendship is dependent on it and subordinate to it. Friendship migrates to where rightness is, and not the other way around.

A similar argument applies in situations where a nation or organization crassly appropriates an ennobling label to itself, but goes on to behave in ways that run counter to the label. "We are democratic, therefore whatever we do has to be seen as democratic." Or even, "Our enterprise is sustainable, therefore whatever we do has to be seen as sustainable." Like the dancing tail of the cat which distracts the prey from what's really going on, the dazzle of the label is supposed to blind all beholders to the real nature of the action in question. The shining tail wags the erring dog.

** *Earth's resources going up in smoke* [18 December, 1998, in the midst of the relentless bombing of Belgrade, Yugoslavia]

As I watch on live television the live bombs raining down and destroying one of the world's cities (Belgrade, Yugoslavia), it is a constant struggle to avoid being mesmerized (as most of the world is) into thinking that this is a movie. I have to strain to remind myself that it is not a Hollywood-produced show. This is not HBO that specializes in movies. This is CNN, bringing its in-your-face coverage of the fury of war live into my home.

What a way for the world's resources to go up in smoke. Millions of dollars have been spent building each missile, while similar millions have been spent building the structures that each missile systematically goes on to destroy on the ground. Both the expensive missile and the valuable structure are reduced to rubble. This is repeated a thousand times, over many days. How many meals for how many mouths in how many countries could these resources have procured for a hungry world?

** *Bombing and Guns* [23 April, 1999, just after the Columbine massacre]

Is there not a connection between the month-long freelance bombing in Yugoslavia and this week's shootings at Columbine High School in Colorado? Both are the products of a gun-crazy, gone crazy, violence-ridden, society whose own arrogance blinds it to its own short-comings.

** *The certainty of Death* [Written on various dates between 8 January 1999 and 29 June 2001]

Should anxiety about eventually having to wake up be allowed to disrupt your deep blissful slumber? Should worries about a future parting make present companionship miserable? Should worries about certain death make your present life wretched?

I have a deadly disease. The doctors say I have had it since the day I was born. It will eventually kill me. Now they tell me I have less than 40 years to live before it gets me. They say there is no cure, but it has a name. It is called *mortis corporis*. Death (of the body). Should I blissfully continue to enjoy my life, or should I be consumed with anxiety about the incurability of my disease?

If, as a youth, you were thrown off an infinitely high cliff that required 65 years before you crash-land, what would be your state of mind in transit? Would you enjoy the ride, or be overwhelmed by anxiety about the disastrous end? It is just like life, where certain demise awaits. Death.

** *Convoluted nature of Life* [15 May 1999]

Life's ultimate purpose seems to be the self-serving mission of nurturing itself and producing more of itself. In all of biology, all living activity seems to have the sole purpose of maintaining life (that already exists) and producing more of life. The whole thing (life) seems to be inextricably turned in on itself. Could the physical universe be somehow similarly turned in on itself?

** *It takes closeness to Death to really appreciate Life* [23 February 2003]

I went to a session on cultural diversity at St. Paul's Methodist (Hilltop) Church, Chambersburg, Pennsylvania. After the Greek wedding film, I led a discussion on diversity. At the end of the session, one woman who was going blind approached me with her husband and said, "If everybody could go through the experience that I am now grappling with (going blind), we would learn how little our differences mattered, and learn to put those differences aside." Very touching. Do we need to be threatened with the withdrawal of the privilege of seeing the differences, for us to see how irrelevant those differences are? Indeed, it takes closeness to death to really appreciate life.

** *The Innocent gets punished for the sins of the Guilty*
[18 July 1999 while living in Papua New Guinea]

Today, Sunday, about 1.30pm. There was a knock outside the door at the house where I lived.

I gave the usual harsh retort, "What do you want?"

Reply from a man outside, "Any job?"

Harsh retort from me, "Nogat!" (none!)

Reply, "I'm willing to work for food."

Harsher retort from me, "Nogat!" (Go, leave me alone!).

All this time, what I did was to retort as harshly as possible, since prior experience had taught me that this was the best way to discourage door-to-door solicitors. I did not go out or peek to see his face, lest he should see mine. Finally, as he retreated towards my neighbor's house, I peeked. It was a young man (early 20's), forlorn, tired looking, and probably quite hungry. He interacted with my neighbor (a PNG national) who eventually gave him water to drink. No food. Maybe he had only asked for water. I felt an urge to go out and offer him a packet of Highway biscuits. But I restrained myself. Too late now. The fellow left my neighbor's compound, then stood listlessly for about five minutes under the shade of a frangipani tree beside the road. Finally, he moved on, probably to another neighbor down the road.

Was he genuinely in need? Probably yes. But unfortunately, he could not be distinguished from all the dishonest fakes that came around. Was my response typical of most people in my neighborhood? Yes. Would he have stolen from me if given the chance? Probably yes.

As he disappeared behind the shrubbery in a far neighbor's area, I could not help but think that the harsh treatment he got from me was due to the character of similar "Painim wok" [job seeker] persons that preceded him. He might have been genuinely in need, but how could you find out or distinguish him from all the others? His possible innocence was obscured by the guilt of the many who preceded him.

I could not help but think of how many times I have received harsh treatment (intrusive searches) from immigration and customs officials in many countries; all because of the unenviable record that some of my compatriots have laid down. Or how racial profiling in the US, based on the statistics of incarceration, has often entrapped innocent black youth going about their business. The innocent does indeed get punished for the sins of the guilty. It is one of the incongruities of collective punishment.

** *Fractals and other Recurring-Problem Metaphors* [13 June 2001]

In my meeting with the Dean today, I found myself ranging from Mathematics to the Liberal Arts and mythology to describe some of the college's problems. Problems that kept recurring after we thought we had solved them. In a metaphor which I originated spontaneously, I first likened such a problem to a graphic fractal, at the end of which new branches emerge, only to end in yet other sets of new branches, ad infinitum. Then I likened the situation to Sisyphus and the stone which he was destined to perpetually roll up the hill. The episode reminded me of the interconnectedness of all branches of knowledge. Both the Sciences and the Arts are rich with useful metaphors.

** *Atemporiasis, the Timelessness disease: I don't have time, do you?* [25 June 2002]

Timelessness (the ubiquitous and chronic lack of time in people's lives) is a disease that I choose to call *Atemporiasis*. It is closely related to the *activity bite syndrome* (as in "sound bites"), where each day is taken up in a large multiplicity of activities, each of them kept deliberately short so that the individual can hurry on to another activity. I cut short my office work so I can attend the meeting in the board room. I leave early from the meeting so I can go listen to the presentation in the auditorium. I abandon the presentation midway, so that I can rush to the bank to discuss my upcoming loan. I can't wait for the bank discussion to reach a meaningful conclusion because it's time to take my cat to the vet.

Each activity is abruptly bookended by another activity, which in turn is bookended by still another activity, in an endless charade of serial bookending. The activities go on and on, each one incompletely or inconclusively performed. The day is littered with scraps of half-performed or unfinished activities. The net effect is that I can credit myself with having performed myriads of activities during that day. But in truth, I only took a bite out of each activity, so that I can hurry off to get a bite out of the next one. I'm like a wary deer browsing in a thicket while in motion: a bite here, a bite there, but moving all the time. The specter of each next activity prevents a meaningful conclusion to the present one. As a result, there is a string of imperfectly concluded activity bites, and the individual is frustrated by the fact that few of the activities reached any satisfying conclusion.

One obvious result of *Atemporiasis* is that most of life is lived at a hurry-hurry pace. And closely allied to that is the equation:

HURRIED = HARRIED

Atemporiasis often comes about when people want to do everything and be everything. The emphasis is on quantity over quality. They avoid the challenging task of prioritization which would force them to draw the line, and to devote their diligence and thoroughness exclusively to the items at the top of the list. They are unwilling to let go the items at the bottom of the list.

Atemporiasis is partially an indirect result of giving up more free time so as to have more possessions. It is more free time versus more possessions wanted. Most people have chosen the latter. The more wants we desire, the more time that is required to generate the resources to meet those wants. Is what you buy worth the extra working hours it will cost you? Would you be willing to work less, earn less, and consume less? Do you suffer from *Atemporiasis*? Uncomplicate your life!

** *It is Pressure that turns Charcoal into Diamond* [30 May 2000, in Lae, Papua New Guinea. Original metaphor used in my speech at the send-off party for the Vice Chancellor, Dr. Kaiulo]

There is charcoal and there is diamond. One is soft, dirty, cheap, and of low value; the other is hard, expensive, and very valuable. But each of them is just carbon, plain and simple. What is it then that enables the dirty inexpensive charcoal carbon to be transformed into the glittering expensive diamond carbon? It is *pressure*. Pressure, exerted over millennia, causes the transformation from charcoal to diamond. Lesson? The pressure put on you is only expediting your transformation from charcoal to diamond, from soft squishiness to cutting-edge toughness. Remember that in the trial by fire (when materials get thrown into fire), chaff and trash get burned up, while silver and gold get refined by fire. Do you place yourself in a position to be combustible chaff or to be refractory gold?

These metaphors are reminiscent of the well-known aphorism: what does not kill you makes you stronger. The oyster, irritated by a grain of sand, responds by producing the most beautiful pearl.

** *Puzzling Logic* [11 August 2001]

Consider the following two convoluted and ambiguous statements and see what you make of them:

*The other day, I found out that I made a mistake. Now I know that I was wrong because I was right.

*The other day, I found out that I made a mistake. Now I know that I was right because I was wrong.

** *Food vs Riches* [2014]

The rich can always find food, but the poor will always feel rich if they have food. The ability to feed yourself is the most valuable of all riches.

This is true for the individual as it is for nations; true for persons as it is for peoples.

** *Have you stopped lying?* [2014]

Here's a case of infinitely convoluted logic. Try to reason through it.

I ask you: Have you stopped lying whenever you answer a question that you're asked?

Answer: No.

This means that you're lying to me now. Since you answered No, the true answer must be Yes. Which means you've stopped lying. If you've stopped lying, then your original answer of No must be correct. In which case, that answer is a lie. Or is it…

** *Kolo's Dilemma: A case of social momentum* [22 March 2001]

Kolo once decided to cut links with his two aunts because he thought that they did not have sufficient regard for him. All efforts by the aunts to maintain the links were rebuffed by Kolo. Nor were they told the reason for the severed links. Eventually, everybody gave up and neither party visited the other. The freeze lasted three years.

Then suddenly one day, Kolo announced that he had decided to resume normal links with his aunts. But to his surprise, the aunts indicated that they were not willing to resume the links until Kolo explained why he ostracized them in the first place. They asked him to remember that when you decide to spin round, the world spins with you. But when you decide to stop, the world does not necessarily stop spinning just then. You have set it in motion, and it tends to want to continue spinning on its own momentum. You can control the onset of the spinning, but you do not have total control over when it stops. So, be careful about starting the spin in the first place. There's a lesson there for social interactions.

** *On Silence* [2014]

Like music where the pause is just as important as the written note; like the car where the brake is just as important as the accelerator; so it is with speech, where silence is just as important as the spoken word.

Judiciously applied, the musical pause, the brake, and silence can be of great and decisive effect.

** *Original Aphorisms* [various dates]

* If you go west far enough, you come out in the east. Just as in politics, the extreme left and extreme right have so much in common. [21 March 2006].

* You're too busy to attend to me…If you cannot make my business part of your busyness, then you have no business with my business.

* Do not pray for a worry-free life. That brand is not available on the shelves of nature's shop. Instead, pray that your shopping cart will be stocked with worries that you can swallow and digest easily; problems that you can surmount. There's plenty of that brand on the shelves. Pray that your God will discipline you but not destroy you; that God will try you but not fry you.

* As you get older, you quickly learn that the physical law of elastic limits applies to many things, including your muscles and your time.

* Dealing with and managing success is just as tricky as dealing with failure. How often do we see people who have succeeded, but allow the success to throw their lives into disarray? A kind of catastrophic success. It's important to know when you've succeeded; then count your blessings and conserve them. As the saying goes, when your cup is full, stop pouring, because any further pouring creates a mess. Similarly, it is important to discern when you have lost; then concede, lick your wounds, and move on.

* It is the goodwill that you build up in times of peace that you draw upon in times of war.

* Stoicism tries to find the middle ground between the jumps of happiness and the lumps of sadness.

* Capitalism has Gross Domestic Product as a measure of societal productivity. Some have modified it to suggest Genuine Progress Indicator (GPI) as a better measure of societal robustness. Bhutan has Gross National Happiness as a measure of societal wellbeing; I propose Gross International Peace (GIP) as a measure of the world's weal. [26 July 2000]

* In the mission of colonization, what was left after the initial salvo of guns was mopped up by the surreptitious salvo of salvation that followed. What the gun could not subdue, the good book did. Silently.

* A free-for-all is never free for all. Some pay a heavy price of injury in the ensuing melee.

* For every person living in decadent opulence, there are dozens who made the same effort but wound up living in decadent decadence. It's all in the cards.

* A knife only gets sharpened by rubbing against a hard object. The same with ideas, which get refined through disputation.

* If you are not in this position, you cannot understand my disposition. [19 September 2000]

* You can be the Devil's Advocate, but please do not be the Devil incarnate.

* Please avoid ultimatums, or else I will you an ultimatum.

* The Fuse Principle: How unique that the weakest point in a system (the fuse) should prove to be its strongest defense.

* It is one thing to be ignorant, and to acknowledge your ignorance. But if you don't know, and don't know that you don't know, then you are the most ignorant person on earth.

* The fact that I can take (tolerate) anything does not mean that I should take anything [12 January 2004].

* One of the most irreverent things is to think that you know the mind of God. This is what breeds religious fanaticism.

* If you chew and swallow your meaty tongue because you are hungry, how will you taste the food when it finally comes? In times of desperation, do not destroy the objects that will aid your ultimate recovery. Don't eat your planting seed stock during the famine.

* There may be an accent in my speaking, but there is no accent in my thinking.

* When a spider anchors its web on the minute hand of a large public clock, the web cannot stand the test of time. It is constantly being disorganized by the passage of time. Build your castles on a firm foundation, not on sand. [26 February 2006].

* God is like Electricity; it needs a bulb (us) for it to shine.
* It is better to be roasted through striving than to be eaten alive. It is better to suffer castigation than to receive retribution without warning.
* While everything in the universe is relative, everything is also *a* relative (i.e. related to us).
* Devote an ounce of contemplation to save a ton of wasted action.
* Nothing is better than [having] something. So, something is better than nothing.
* The hallowed distance between amity and calamity can be quite short in some places [30 June 1997].
* However big the piece of meat that the [West African] fufu bolus manages to pick up from the soup, it (bolus) must be dispossessed of the meat before it (bolus) journeys down the throat. (Bolus = man; meat = wealth; throat = the death passage). So it is that however substantial the riches that you've picked up in your life, you will be stripped of them as you make your way through the narrow passage of death. As the popular saying goes, you cannot take it with you. [25 January 1998].
* The pains of idleness: It is bad enough to be doing nothing; but the only thing worse than doing nothing is having nothing to do. [21 April 1999].
* *Promises* should always be RAW: Redeemed, Amended, or Withdrawn. Never leave a promise dangling without subjecting it to RAW. Otherwise, avoid making the promise in the first place. [25 March 2013].
* Silence is to Speech what contemplation is to religious expression.
* Whatever the original color of your hair (black, blonde, red), the pressures of life and time have the same effect on it: it turns gray. [12 October 2002]. (Just like: whatever your skin color, we are all the same color when the lights go out).
* Three concepts that mankind should strive to make obsolete are: Enemy, War and Waste.
* Magnanimity and mercy motivate the mighty, but not the mean.
* Impulse can lead to the most enjoyable sex; but it also can lead to the most regrettable sex.

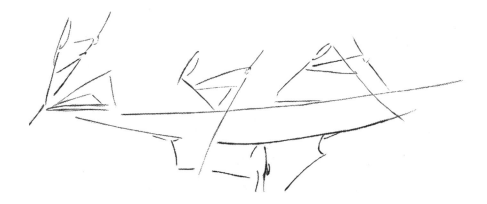

SECTION D:

UNASKED QUESTIONS
Driving the American Ethos:
Enter poetic sarcasm

Context: This nine-part epic poem uses tongue-in-cheek sarcasm to critically examine the American national and personal ethos. Its message is central to the theme of this book. Not surprisingly, it lends its title, in modified form, to be the overall title of the book. It is written in the couplet style made so famous by Chaucer. Many of the couplets frame questions that people rarely ask, but which desperately need to be asked. Certain themes already touched on in prose are revisited for poetic treatment from a different perspective. This poem was written and copyrighted in 2006, in Springfield, Missouri, USA.

UNASKED QUESTIONS DRIVING THE AMERICAN ETHOS

I. INTRODUCTION

Don't bother me, I'm enjoying the good life;
Me, my children, my dog, my husband or wife.
We've got our job of living well to pursue,
Surfeit of things inconceivable by you;
Big cars, gadgets, houses, no caution heeded;
More and more things, goods, needed and unneeded.
Those not needed, we squirrel away and store,
So that we can make room to bring in some more.
We just can't wait to rush down to the grand mall
To fill attics full with trivia big and small.
We're told it is our civic contribution,
To consume lots, to prop up our great nation.
That's how, they say, our purse is well fortified.
That's how we keep our enemies mystified.

While I revel in all bliss and consumption
I find my time depleted to exhaustion.
I have no time high profound things to pursue;
Can I sub-let my conscience over to you?
No time for thought, less time for introspection
Just tell me how to vote in next election.
Think for me please, plan for me, and war for me,
Digest the news in weather calm or stormy
Then allow your vapid vomit to guide me
You say I'm naught unless you're there beside me.
Like fledgling bird to whom loving mother flies,
Feed me false news, your pre-digest of big lies,
And when you've made your cold-blooded decisions,
Tell me what thoughts to think to push your visions.

Bathe me with thoughts that I'm by far superior
To all mankind, who are somehow inferior.
They're to serve me, they're there to do my bidding,
I'm to lead them to walk my way, no kidding.
My sense is one of grandiose entitlement
From distant lands and from our own government.
My nation is God's gift to all of mankind.
All of the gold, all resources that you'll find,
Be it right here, be it in the foreign lands,
All must serve me, my people, and our own ends.
Our ego's starved, it is a must to lead it
To other lands whose lot is just to feed it.

II. OUR TRAITS

Our prized system is perfect to the letter,
Can't improve it, man can't do any better.
Ordained from high, it's simply the very best
That's no boasting, no vain pounding of the chest.
We're just so good, why can't others accept it?
It's a secret, and we're the ones who kept it.
If they resist, we must cajole and bully.
We must insist that they be brought round fully
To understand that we've discerned perfection,
Our great system deserves their rapt affection.

Other systems are deemed not permissible,
No other way is allowed compatible.
We'll denigrate, continually despoil them,
Discern their ways and plans so we can foil them.
If we have to, we'll *demonize and destroy.*
It is one trick we very often employ.
And if it fails, we'll take the mantle higher
We'll raise the stakes, and blast them in our ire.

"Demonizer" describes our serial function
As we lambaste, ignoring all compunction.
The pressure stays till they come to their senses
And see their world only through our grand lenses.
And all this while, we love many a devil
Whose sins are great, regimes equally evil.
We do not mind their great multitude of sins
If they support us and guarantee our wins.

Some say let be, let us have diverse systems.
Live and let live, there's room for many items.
Nature itself depends on diversity
To let evolve in great multiplicity
All living things that you can well imagine,
As mooted by no less a man than Darwin.
Diversity of systems leads to progress
A lack of it, and we'll surely retrogress.
When we insist on just our one single way,
Do we plant seeds of the earth's future decay?

There are great truths that govern my existence,
Values held dear values worth all insistence
Not just by me but by compatriot brothers
Values we love, values we foist on others.
Values we push without much hesitation
In hopes they'll grow to be just like our nation.

Here are the traits that mostly shape our life's ways:
Victory is one, which means we must win always;
Other key words are *Strength*, and sheer *Toughness*, too;
And being *First*, setting great records anew.
And then there's *Fun*, yes fun in everything done.
Ne'er mind results, focus on having much fun.
Then don't forget, *Patriotism* there too.
These things guide us, at least they seem so to do.
Now let us look and examine in detail
How they play out when looked upon in full scale.

III. VICTORY

Victory's a trait we cherish with a passion
Be it in war, in games and all transaction.
Key word is *"win"*, even lose all to do it.
Must win, must win, or else you'll live to rue it.
Sometimes we just declare victory and then stop,
When all can see we have simply given up.
Such is the need to wear the cloak of victory
Who cares a hoot if the cloak is transitory?
Is borrowed cloak, even if a threadbare shawl,
Not better than our having no cloak at all?

The sages say that winning's not all glory.
Each one who's won leaves one that's feeling sorry.
Does each winner not perforce yield a loser?
Loss and victory than brothers are much closer.
Jubilation to ululation's bonded
Like snail and shell eternally compounded;
Like hand and glove, like baked bread and butter do,
Like sea and sky, like live fish and water too.

Winners rejoice, crassly flaunting their good luck
While losers grieve their fate, wallowing in muck.
Where victory's grown to be a potent totem,
Should we discard losers or trample on them?
While victors dance in their high lofts secluded,
What do we do with those victory's eluded?

IV. STRENGTH

Strength is a trait that certainly defines us.
It's one true bond that in everything binds us.
Our leaders plot, exploit our dear love for Strong,
"If you are strong, no way that you can be wrong."
They project strength even for wrongful causes
Hoping we'll clap and give them our applauses.
They know that we when given the chance to choose
Between Rightness or Strength even if obtuse,
We'll go for Strength because we hold it dearly
Our love for Strength beats that for Rightness clearly.
We just confirm the song they use in their fight,
"Better be strong and wrong, than be weak and right."

With "Strong" so strong it sure is no great surprise
That it begets ideologies of big lies
Such modes of thought recalcitrant to changing
E'en when logic shows things need rearranging.
When thoughts of Strong are in such sturdy command
Is there a place for the weak folks in our land?

V. DEMOCRACY

In global terms, we like to show we're strong too,
Even in spheres where it would just be wrong to.
We do not care if it's abomination,
We must show all our sense of domination.
Tell all others just what they will need to do
To keep us glad, or else we will make them stew.
We castigate them for will to be different.
How dare they think outside our declared intent?
Democracy! That is our favorite war cry;
We do not care whether you will laugh or cry.
Just you concede that it is what we practice
Huge flaws and all, and everything that's amiss.

Consider well the last couple centuries
It does not take the craft of judge and juries
To well discern the world's most blatant scourges.
Right here's a list of mankind's greatest blotches:
Slavery is one, colonialism is two,
Communism, imperialism's there too,
Racist ethos, exemplified by Nazis
And their good friends who called themselves the Axis.
It's clear to note these stains without exception,
The apogee of man to man deception,
Have all been wrought by people of our own kin
Here or yonder; they're guilty of serious sin.
You may then ask, with such a history blighted
With so much shame, how can we stay delighted?
What claim have we to much moral uppity,
When we've been part of such crass iniquity?
How placed are we to gird ourselves in flowers
To don white robes and preach from lofty towers?
We forget that despite great proclamation,
It took us two hundred years as a nation
Before something near human equality

179

Could rear its head, and attain legality.
Even since then it's drawn much perspiration
To actualize the tardy legislation.
How do others think of us when for so much
Of our history we've had such a perverse touch?
Evil enthroned and outright subjugation,
Sometimes even conscious annihilation
Of native peoples and those deemed less than human.
We've trampled them, made them less man or woman.

If it's taken so long with our resources
For us to rid ourselves of all these vices,
To get our vain imperfect act together,
How placed are we to vilify the other
Nations that are still struggling and still fledgling,
Some with just few decades of nation-building?
Given the faults that our system does well show
Where's our right to pontificate, proudly crow?
Can you foster democracy's existence
Through use of force, dictatorial insistence?
How can we hope to use autocracy's tool
As a fair means to spread democracy's pool?
Autocracy serves democracy. Not nice;
It's but a sham, like seeking virtue through vice.

Democracy, we shout to judge and jury,
But we insist on veto vote *de jure*;
Or *de facto* as we cruise round the whole globe
Throwing our weight to rein in and cow the mob.
We shout "Reform!" when other lands are concerned,
But for ourselves zero reforms we intend.
Democracy, if it's so good for persons,
Why can't it work in organizing nations?

VI. ARMAMENT

The drive for Strong leads us in all directions
Like how we see global armamentations.
We build up arms and spend lots to fine-tune them
They give us heft and we in turn festoon them.
But we cry foul should some other nations try
To match our arms or even to ask us why.

Our people boast we have many troops deployed
All o'er the world, and for that we're overjoyed.
Build bases here, build some barracks over there;
Got soldiers there, got our airmen everywhere.
No one questions so much exported terror;
No one dares ask, could all this be in error?
There is yet one other question worth asking:
Of all the lands, the countries where we're basking,
Our troop deployed, our bases aptly maintained,
Commandos there with broad powers unrestrained,
Which ones of them have their troops based in our land?
Which have our troops under their captain's command?
Virtually none, that's the honest true reply.
Then you must ask, is there a good reason why?
Is it ordained, predestined, immutable,
Our armies deemed for ever to be able
To occupy their lands and make all the fuss,
While they in turn cannot do the same to us?
How would we feel if foreign armies camped out
All o'er our lands and built huge fortresses stout?
If you believe that it is unthinkable
For foreign folks to rise and turn the table,
Then spare a thought for patriots of those nations
Who see us there in one-sided equations,
Where we inflict upon them such affliction
That they can do to us only in fiction.

Will this status, with so much inequity,
This imbalance that is cause for much pity,
Make them love us, embrace us in their arms, or
Make them hate us, despising us more and more?

VII. SUPER ARMAMENT

Let's look again at the armament question
For which I said we are a major bastion.
Please contemplate the ultimate in weapon
That mankind's set his warped crooked mind upon.
Yes I speak of the feared nuclear weapons myth
Which most nations now seek to gird themselves with.
It is a myth because long-term projection
Tells us it's just delusory protection.
It's a genie that has escaped the bottle,
It's gone rampant, its power hard to scuttle.
Sorry it's done, but what's our solution now?
The genie must be tamed, and we must find how.
How can nations avoid this sweet seduction,
This opium of mutual assured destruction?
As long as one earth's nation has the poison
Others will strive to get it and that quite soon.
Best antidote to nuke proliferation
Is some progress within each nuclear nation
Relinquishing the poison that they have now.
While you have it, you just cannot tell me how
You can convince others to stay far from it,
Or to open for inspections and permit.
Yet what we see in all the world's alarming;
It opens up our fate to future harming.
The nations that have nuke arms and can stew it,
Patrol the waves making sure you don't brew it;
While all the time assiduous in their searching
To maximize its punch through their researching.
Can a nation with nuke stuff that does love it
Morally preach to others not to have it?
For all the world, they seemingly say to you,
"Do as I say, but do not do as I do."
One yardstick's there for you when I will measure,
Different yardstick for me to keep my treasure.

This principle extends to many a sphere
Like subsidies, like arms sales to everywhere.

Is it not clear that by far the greatest force
Pushing nations to nuke arms is the huge farce
Where those with it continue to improve it,
Guarding it well, refusing to remove it?
And worse than that they do refuse to foreswear
Their will to use it whene'er a threat is near.
In such a case of clear intimidation
Other nations balk at their limitation.
If I can keep my dagger and prevent you
From getting one or having one be lent you,
Do we not lay roots of long term suspicion
Between persons, between nation and nation?
Is possible cohabitation stable
When one is armed, the other vulnerable?

Let us recall the world's most recent history
In times gone by but of recent memory;
How it was that today's real geopolitics
Was made to be through great treachery and tricks.
Those that had guns, emboldened by their weapon
Found the unarmed so easy to prey upon.
With guns on them it was an easy option
To subjugate each gun-less native nation.
In North and South of land of America
Australia too, and also in Africa.
Most of Asia did suffer the same sorrow:
Hapless natives fighting with bow and arrow.
Their fate was sealed, their fortunes clearly undone.
They were no match for the intruders with gun.
T'was the secret of the earth's conquistadors.
They did not care for ethics or pious mores.
They used the gun on those who couldn't make it;
They clung to it, they would not dare forsake it.

Now let us ask, in modern times of today,
In the space age, what great weapon shall we say
Stands in the place that's equivalent to guns,
Giving nations huge capacity that stuns?
It seems so clear, to use the new metaphor,
The nuke weapon equates the old gun for sure.
Those who have it do not have any intent
To give it up, instead they are truly bent
On cradling it, using it at their pleasure
To dominate and corral all earth's treasure.
Small nations cringe and cower, shaking in fear
That just as guns subdued ancestors earlier,
The nuclear thing, today's gun, is a potion
To foist on them perpetual subjugation.
That's why they all keep striving hard to invent
Nuke arms of theirs while hiding their real intent.

Let us suppose the world woke up tomorrow
And found itself so much relieved from sorrow
With nuclear states giving up nuclear weapons,
Razing for good all their stockpiled megatons.
In such a case, would it not be much clearer,
More practical and surely so much fairer,
To persuade all those we call rogue nations
To put away their crass nuclear ambitions?
So long as big nations do their double-speak,
So long also small nations play hide-and-seek.
India today, tomorrow it's Pakistan;
Libya today, tomorrow it is Iran;
Another time, focus is on North Korea;
In future time maybe it is Liberia.
Is it not clear that as mankind grows knowledge,
Some in the lab and some in every college,
More nations will acquire know-how needed
To go to nuclear the way others succeeded?
We will just have endless proliferations

Of those we choose to label as rogue nations.

Just by the way, it's possible to define
The tag of "Rogue" along a different line:
Could the real rogues be those monopolizing
Mankind's demon, for use in demonizing?

Meanwhile all things, people in every nation,
Are threatened with total annihilation.
Wisdom tells us the only way to save us
From this poison that mankind has in service
Is for all lands to demolish piece by piece
Their nuke weapons, and leave the good earth in peace.

VIII. PATRIOTISM

And so it is with strong addiction to Strong,
Also Winning a potent coequal prong,
We surge ahead, not caring whose ox is gored;
We ride along, cavalier mixed with roughshod.
One art that we have mastered to perfection
Is the great art of *enemy-creation*.
This art sure gets our dear people energized
That's one reason why it is so highly prized.
There're enemies upon which they can focus
To vent their spleen and pour out their bitter cuss.
It helps deflect a lot of their attention
From the defects in our system and nation.
Find enemies whatever be the reason,
From year to year, for season after season.
For reasons big or reasons that are paltry
We find a foe in country after country.
At various times it was the USSR.
At other times it is simply Myanmar.
China's been there, so too has good old Libya
Cuba, Iraq, then also count Somalia.
The list goes on although changing with the years
Constantly sure to pique our own people's fears.
Any country whose leader dares to stand up
To call our bluff then they will simply wind up
On our black list of bad enemies for sure.
They'll bear the brunt of the heat we have in store.
The tool we use to cause maximum mayhem:
We make our folks think it is *"us versus them."*
We stoke fires of crass *patriotism,*
The kind that is quite close to nepotism;
The kind that says and dishes out the order
That love and trust should stop smack at the border.
If for our land, patriotism's surfeit,
Cannot we have a pan-human brand of it?

One where any part of all humanity
That is challenged with any adversity
Draws attention for all human beings to see
It as their task wherever they may now be.
Since borders are creations made by mankind,
They should be crossed by the patriotic mind.

When you proclaim your country's the very best
While others think perhaps it might be the worst
Do you expect others to simply accept
All that you say because it is your precept?
It is like one who projects his own mother
Convincing all she betters any other.
We all concede to you your mother's goodness
Even grant her perfection to the fullness.
Problems arise if you proceed to define
Your mother as being much better than mine.
So it is with great patriotism too.
Your country's great, I will concede that to you.
But don't be crass, rubbing it all in my face,
Denigrating my country with sour disgrace.
Please love your land but do not try to force me
To love your own more than mine, or to boss me.
In any case, the love of any country
Should ne'er exceed the love of humanity.
The former is an artificial creature
The latter is creation wrought by nature.

IX. CONCLUSION

So, I am chic, but my sophistication
Lies in great fun, not in great rumination.
There are others out there, but I'm too busy
Enjoying life, the fun just makes me dizzy.
You say I could improve the situations
By seeking clues to some of the big questions.
Questions till now we all left unattended.
Further I hear the way your advice ended:
Worse than questions left unanswered from the past
Is the huge pile of questions not being asked.
If you don't pose tough questions as aforesaid,
Who do you think will then ask them in your stead?

Other books by Prof. Inno Chukuma ONWUEME

[Available at Amazon, Google Books, etc.]

1. *Like A Lily Among Thorns: Colonial African village child transitions to post-colonial modernity, and America.* Author House 2014. 348pp. [Readers' Favorite FIVE-STAR winner 2014]. http://bookstore.authorhouse.com/Products/SKU-000678459/Like-A-Lily-Among-Thorns.aspx

2. *Auction In Zunguzonga: Sustainable Development Deferred.* Author House, 2005. 206pp. http://bookstore.authorhouse.com/Products/SKU-000357077/Auction-In-Zunguzonga.aspx

3. *Okita Okita: Tales about Anioma culture in Africa.* 1st Books Publishers, 2001. 104pp. [Winner, *Writer's Digest* MERIT AWARD, 2002]

4. *Taro cultivation in Asia and the Pacific.* FAO (United Nations Food & Agricultural Organization) RAP Publication: 1999/16.

5. *The kava crop and its potential.* United Nations FAO, RAP Publication 1997/12. [with M.Papademetriou]

6. *Tropical Root and Tuber Crops: Production, Perspectives, and Future Prospects.* United Nations FAO, Rome. 1994. 228pp. [with W.B.Charles]

7. *Agrometeorology and Eco-physiology of Cassava.* Monograph for the World Meteorological Organization, Geneva, Switzerland. 1993

8. *Field Crop Production in Tropical Africa.* CTA, Wageningen, Netherlands. 1991. 480pp. [with T.D.Sinha]

9. *General Agriculture & Soils.* (editor). Cassell Ltd. London. 1982. 102pp. [with E.A.Aduayi & E.E.Ekong]

10. *Animal Science.* (editor) Cassell Ltd. London 1981. 105pp. [with G.Ositelu]

11. *Crop Science.* Cassell Ltd. London. 1979. 106pp.

12. *The Tropical Tuber Crops: yams, cassava, sweet potato, cocoyams.* John Wiley & Sons, Chichester, UK. 1978. 234pp.

Printed in the United States
By Bookmasters